COLLECTOR'S GUIDE TO CARTOON & PROMOTIONAL DRINKING GLASSES

BY JOHN HERVEY

Second Printing
1992

PUBLISHED BY
L-W BOOK SALES
P.O. BOX 69
GAS CITY, IN 46933

About The Author

John Hervey has been a collector all his life. During his grade school years he collected coins from his paper route money. Then he graduated to antique radios and early wireless equipment since he is in the electronic business. In his 20's he also collected early light bulbs that dated back to 1895 that still worked which he still has. Have you heard the saying, "The only thing that separates the men from the boys is the cost of their toys." So in his thirty's he collected, bought and sold Midyear Corvettes. Then as that was winding down he was at a flea market one day and picked up a glass and wondered who collects these. You hear about them on TV and in the fast food restaurants but who does it. With no books on the market he along with Miles Bader Published the first book on cartoon glasses. Other credits include articles for antique papers on glasses along with television appearance in Dallas for glasses, radios and light bulbs. The most recent publications include a quarterly newsletter on glasses called "Glass Collector Update" and he also publishes, "The Collectors Check List Guide on Glasses".

How To Use This Book

Trying to come up with a way to catalog glasses has been one of the most challenging areas of this project. If you were doing a book for collectors only, then that would make the job a lot easier. My goal was to design a system that could be used by antique dealers, flea market vendors and collectors. I have tried to be very simple, yet design a system that would grow as the glass collection grew.

Looking through the index you will see seven categories. They are Coca Cola, Disney, Holly Hobby, McDonalds, Pepsi Cola, Norman Rockwell, and the Wizard of Oz. The number one preference is PEPSI COLA. If the glass has a Pepsi logo on it, then it goes under that category. Pepsi was the largest sponsor of cartoon glasses in the 1970's. The other categories, like McDonalds have all the McDonalds glasses alphabetized under that category unless they have a Pepsi logo. The same example applies to Walt Disney. The Walt Disney glasses with a Pepsi logo will appear under Pepsi, not Walt Disney. However, if the glass is one they sponsored without a bottling company, then it appears under Walt Disney. This means that a Pepsi logo takes priority over any other catagory. The rest of the index is arranged so that when you pick up a glass and it has the Baltimore Orioles on it you will find it under what it is, Baltimore. The same holds true with others such as King Kong, Howdy Doody, Popeye, Star Trek and so on.

Each set of glasses has it's own set #, which consists of the first letter of the glass or a combination of letters that would give you an idea of what series of glasses you wan to look up. Example, the first set is Alaska Historical Series, Set # AHS. All of the Walt Disney start with WD in front of them, then the next two or three letters like AW have something to do with the description of the glass. Example, Alice in Wonderland, Set #WDAW. The number to the left of the brackets is the glass number to the set. Example Daisy and Donald in the 1977 set of Pepsi Happy Birthday Mickey would be P for Pepsi, HBM for Happy Birthday Mickey and 1 for the glass number, PHBM1.

We have tried to make the catalog system workable for everyone. Realizing that not everyone is as familiar with the glasses, you can find them both numerically and alphabetically. We left enough room for any set to be able to grow without destroying the set number. When a new set is issued, a new set number will be created along with any glasses in that set. Likewise, if another glass is found to an existing set, all we do is add the glass number to that set.

All reference material has its own way of working and this book is no different. Once you use the system, you will find it really makes identifying any glass very easy.

Forward

People often ask me how long ago did glass collecting start and the best answer I can give them is that it must have started when the first cartoon or promotional glasses were manufactured. My oldest documented glasses are 1932. They were made by an unknown glass source and have the characters of an old vaudeville play on them. They can be seen in this book under the name of the illustrator, John Held Jr. Most of the early glasses that people will find or recognize will be produced by The Libbey Glass Company with Walt Disney Characters on them.

The first full length animated movie was Snow White and Seven Dwarfs, aired on December 21, 1937. To promote the movie, Libbey and Disney put the movie characters on the newly styled "safe edge tumblers". Variety stores sold the glasses or you could get them free with the purchase of cream cheese or cottage cheese at the food stores. Local dairies across the United States joined in the promotion which saved Libbey Glass from the same depression as the country.

After the Snow White and Seven Dwarfs promotion was winding down, Disney released the second full-length animated feature film in 1938, Pinocchio. The Pinocchio glasses were not as popular as Snow White which makes them more difficult to find and higher priced.

For the next 12 years Disney continued producing more films. They continued to feature characters such as Mickey, Minnie, Horace Horse Collar and many others. Most of these characters were shown individually on glass or in glass sets of two.

In 1953 Welches decided to feature the popular Howdy Doody characters and scenes on their jelly glasses (jars). The promotion met with such success that they repeated the promotions using other popular characters from the 1960's, such as the Flintstones, Superman and Mr. Magoo.

Then in the mid to late 1960's fast food restaurants started to appear. To promote their restaurants they joined with the soft drink bottlers like Pepsi, Coke and Dr. Pepper to develop a marketing plan. This combined effort resulted in glasses featuring popular cartoon characters like Superman, Batman, Robin, Aquaman and Wonderwoman. Eventually, the success of the marketing plan gave way to more and more fast food chains offering promotional glasses. Whatever characters were popular at the time soon appeared on glasses, including Harvey Cartoons', Richie Rich, Casper and Baby Huey. MGM's characters included Barney, Spike and Jerry. P.A.T. Ward's Boris and Natasha, Rockey and Bullwinkle.

Major restaurant chains such as McDonalds, Burger King, Sonic Drive-In, and Taco Bell continued to be an excellent avenue for companies to distribute promotional glasses. In addition to glasses, some restaurants have added other items such as plastic toys, cups and mugs. Even gasoline stations have participated, often with sports teams featured on glasses.

Because these items are issued regionally, collectors have a real challenge finding some items. What may be in abundance in your area may not have been issued in someone elses. Networks of collectors have formed in the United States and Canada to buy, sell and trade items. Several people now conduct auctions of glasses. Prices will vary depending on availability, condition, age and how bad you want it! This hobby can be fun, interesting and sometimes frustrating when you're trying to find that last glass in the set.

As of the writing of this book I have over 1800 different cartoon and promotional glasses. I also have over 7000 glasses in stock to use as trade material. When you get this many glasses, the hobby does become serious.

Good Luck and Happy Hunting.
John Hervey

Explanations of Abbreviations

BTM: means bottom, such as rd. btm. or creased btm.

BROCKWAY: a thick heavy glass that tapers in from top to bottom.

CREASED: a glass that has a indentation (ind.) at the base of the glass, but the glass returns toi its normal outer diameter before it reaches the bottom (btm.)

FEDERAL GLASS: a thin straight sided glass that is the same diameter from top to bottom.

FLARE: normally associated with coca cola flare glasses. Big flare at the top of the glass.

FLARE, SLIGHT: Normally associated with ET glasses.

HEAVY BASE: a glass that normally has ¼" to ½" inch thick glass at the base. Like a S.O.R. glass.

IND. BASE: indented base, normally creased in at the bottom of the glass and doesn't return to its outer diameter.

PED. BASE: pedestal base.

RD. BTM.: round bottom, glass doesn't have straight sides and turns in approximately ½" top and bottom.

S.S.: straight sides, a glass that has straight sides and could have any combinations of bases.

S.O.R.: scotch on the rocks, glass that is approximately 4" to 5" in height and has s.s. and a heavy base.

Paint and Glass Restoration

To check the amount of fade in the paint, turn the glass around and look at the paint from the back side. That will give you an idea of how much the paint has faded and the thickness of the paint. If the paint looks to be thin or you can see through it, then I don't recommend using any abrasive to clean it.

A good glass grinder can get rid of small chips in and around the rim.

You can restore the luster of the paint and get rid of some of the water spots first by cleaning the glass of all dirt. Let the glass dry completely then dip glass into a solution of three parts mineral spirits to one part of clear polyurathane. Invert glass on drainer to dry over night. The mineral spirits will evaporate off over night and leave a smooth deposit of clear polyurathane on the glass. You will be very pleased with the results. The solution can't be stored for very long, so I recommend you have several glasses to do before mixing the solution.

Please do not try to pass a restored glass to a collector.

Price Guide for Collector Glasses

This guide will give you some idea of the value of the collector series glasses. A fair market value is based on the following criteria:
(1) Scarcity   (2) Popularity   (3) Condition.

For a glass to bring the highest price it must be in mint condition and none of the following may be present.

1. No defects in the glass
2. No scratches or chips
3. All colors within the lines
4. No smudges in paint, all paint within the lines
5. No faded colors
6. No dishwasher spots or stains

The Price Code is the Number to the Right of the Brackets

Price # Code	Approximate Value
0	$ 1.00 – 2.00
1	$ 3.00 – 5.00
2	$ 6.00 – 10.00
3	$ 10.00 – 20.00
4	$ 20.00 – 30.00
5	$ 30.00 – 50.00
6	$ 50.00 – 70.00
7	$ 70.00 – 90.00
8	$ 90.00 – 120.00
9	$120.00 – 150.00
10	$150.00 – Up

Please note that because most glasses are regional, this too could have an effect on the price of a glass. Your personal desire for a glass can also reflect a higher price paid. We have tried not to let auction prices affect our judgement on the value of glasses, but to list a fair market value.

Acknowledgements

I would like to thank the following people for their support in this book.

Linda Hervey, my wife, for putting up with my long hours. Les and Beverly Chapman for housing me and taking me all around the LA area to hunt for glasses. Melva Davern, thanks for trading with me some of your prize possessions, good luck on your book. Carolyn Markowski, thanks for your input and knowledge on glasses, good luck on your book. Robert Moring, thanks for letting me photograph part of your collection, especially geezil and castor oil. Miles Bader for the start on the check list and being one of the first glass pioneers. David Cole for your knowledge and searching out new sets. Barrie Williamson for trading and sending glasses to photograph. BWC Photo Labs thanks for the extra help on the photographs and putting up with an amature photographer.

Glass Grading

I don't know if there is anything harder, grading a glass or trying to catalog them. Collectors are very particular about the condition of the glasses they have in their collections. If you are selling or trading glasses, the condition of the glass is equally important.

There are three things you have to look at when grading a glass, whether for your collection, or to trade/sell with another collector.
1. The condition of the glass.
2. The condition of the paint and register. (Paint within the lines)
3. Water spots, stains, fading or dulling.

Below is an explanation of what collectors will expect.

Glass Condition List

Mint: glass must be flawless. No chips or scratches. All paint must be within the lines with no signs of fading or discoloration. No smudging of paint within the lines. No dishwasher spots or stains.

Excellent: glass must be in good condition. It may have a bubble or some imperfection in it, but very slight. No chips or scratches. There should be no fading of paint or paint out of line, but paint may be on the line. No smudging of paint within the lines. No dishwasher spots or stains.

Good: glass may have some noticeable imperfections. No chips or scratches. Some of the paint may be out of the lines. There may be some small spots of paint missing. Paint may have lost some of its gloss. Some smudging of paint may be present. There may be slight signs of dishwasher spots and stains.

Poor: glass will have some noticeable imperfections. Small chips may be present in the rim or glass may be warped and out of shape. Base may be sagging. Paint will be out of line and there will be fading more than 10 to 15 percent. There also may be smudging, dishwasher spots and stains.

TABLE OF CONTENTS

ALASKA HISTORICAL SERIES – Set #AHS
Kentucky Fried Chicken (1977) – Rey Corp.
Rd. Btm. 5 5/16"

1	2	3	4	5	6

Alaska State Flag/Flower/Bear/Bird . . . . 1( )2
Eskimo & Husky . . . . 2( )2
Gold Miners . . . . 3( )2

Mt. McKinley . . . . 4( )2
Pruoltoe Bay . . . . 5( )2
Totem/Russian/Ship/Church . . . . 6( )2

ANIMAL CRACKERS – Set #ACR
(1978) Chicago Tribune – Crease at Btm. 6 1/6"

1	2	3	4

5	6

Dodo . . . . 1( )2
Eugene . . . . 2( )2
Gnu . . . . 3( )2
Lana . . . . 4( )2
Louis . . . . 5( )2
Lyle . . . . 6( )2

ANIMAL SERIES II – Set #ANS
No logos or sponsors – 5⅝" S.S. Heavy Base

1   2   3   1   2   3

Full Back/Hippo #21 – Tan Character,
   red/white helment . . . . 1( )2
Offensive Guard/Skunk #23 – Black/white,
   red/white helment . . . . 2( )2
Red Dog / Dog #22 – Red Dog, Tan/white helment . 3( )2

ANIMAL SPORTS – Set #ASG
No logos mfg. by Bartlett Collins Glass Co.

3   2   1   4

Freddie Flamingo . . . . 1( )2
Kid Koala . . . . 2( )2
Match Point Mert . . . . 3( )2
Parallel Panda . . . . 4( )2

APOLLO SERIES – Set #APO
Libbey Glass Co. – Ind. Btm.

1   2   3   4

6

Man On The Moon #11 . . . . 1( )1
Return To The Moon #12 . . . . 2( )1
Safe Return #13 . . . . 3( )1
Alan Shepard Jr. #14 . . . . 4( )1
Moonshot Spaceship (1969) . . . . 5( )1
Pitcher Came With Set . . . . 6( )1

ARBY'S BICENTENNIAL – Set #ARB
(1976) Brockway Glasses – Mixture of TTV,
Pat Ward, Harvey Cartoon, Walter Lantz

1-11-12

2-13

3-14-15

4-16

5-17

6-18

7-19

8-20

9-21 10-22

	16 oz. Thick	11 oz.
Bullwinkle (Crossing the Delaware) Yellow Flag		11( )2
Bullwinkle (Crossing the Delaware) Red Flag	1( )3	12( )3
Bullwinkle (Defense of Country) .	2( )3	13( )3
Casper and Nightmares – Black Hat and verse	3( )3	14( )3
Casper and Nightmares – Blue Hat and verse		15( )3
Dudley Takes Tea (Boston Tea Party)	4( )3	16( )3
George by Woody	5( )2	17( )3
Hot Stuff and Patriot	6( )2	18( )3
Never Fear – Underdog	7( )3	19( )3
Rocky In the Dawns Early Light .	8( )3	20( )3
Underdog Saves Bell (Liberty Bell) .	9( )3	21( )3
Woody Has Spirit	10( )3	22( )3

ARBY'S CHRISTMAS (HOLLY & BERRIES) – Set #ARC

(1983) 5" Tumbler – Inward Slope . . . . 1( )1
(1984) 5" Tumbler – Inward Slope . . . . 2( )1
(1985) 6¾" Stemware – Slight Flare . . . . 3( )1
(1986) 6¾" Stemware – Slight Flare . . . . 4( )1
(1987) 5¾" Tumbler – Slight Flare . . . . 5( )1
(1987) 6¾" Stemware – Slight Flare . . . . 6( )1

3   4   6

ARBY'S MONOPOLY – Set #ARM
4¾" Heavy Base S.O.R. Glass (1985)

1   2   3   4

Collect . . . . 1( )3
Jail . . . . 2( )3
Parking . . . . 3( )3
Visiting . . . . 4( )3

ARBY'S ZODIAC – Set #ARZ
Brockway 16 oz. – 6 5/16"

1   9   11

Aquarius	. . . .	1( )1
Aries	. . . .	2( )1
Cancer	. . . .	3( )1
Capricorn	. . . .	4( )1
Gemini	. . . .	5( )1
Leo	. . . .	6( )1
Libra	. . . .	7( )1
Pisces	. . . .	8( )1
Sagittarius	. . . .	9( )1
Scorpio	. . . .	10( )1
Taurus	. . . .	11( )1
Virgo	. . . .	12( )1

ARBY'S MISCELLANEOUS – Set #ARX

1   3   5

5¼" Rd. Sloped Ped. – Tiffany	1( )1
6" Rd. Sloped Ped. – Tiffany	2( )1
6½" Stars and Stripes (1976) – Slight Flare . . .	3( )1
Pitcher	4( )1
Arby's logo around a bell shaped glass 5⅛" . . .	5( )1

ARCHIES – Set #ARE
(1971) Welches Jelly Co. – 8 oz. 4 3/16"

1   2   3   4

5

6

ARCHIES – Set #ARH
Welches Jelly Co. – 4 3/16"

1

2

3

4

5

6

Faces in bottom of glasses are: Archie, Veronica, Sabrina, Jughead, Hot Dog, Mr. Weatherbee, Reggie and Blank.

ARIZONA CACTUS GLASSES – Set #ARI
(1959) Blakely Gas Station

9-17   16-24

	6½" Clear	6½" Frost	3¾" Frost
Barrel	1( )3	9( )2	17( )2
Century Plant	2( )3	10( )2	18( )2
Cholla	3( )3	11( )2	19( )2
Ocotillo	4( )3	12( )2	20( )2
Organ Pipe	5( )3	13( )2	21( )2
Prickly Pear	6( )3	14( )2	22( )2
Saguaro	7( )3	15( )2	23( )2
Yucca	8( )3	16( )2	24( )2

Wooden carrier / branding iron design (10)

AROUND THE WORLD – Set #ATW
(1960)

Canada	1( )1	Italy	6( )1
England	2( )1	Japan	7( )1
France	3( )1	Mexico	8( )1
Germany	4( )1	Spain	9( )1
Hawaii	5( )1	USA	10( )1

BALTIMORE ORIOLES – Set #BLO
(1984) 6" Rd. / Flare Rim

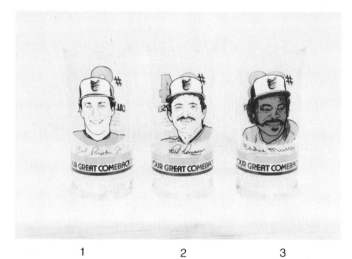

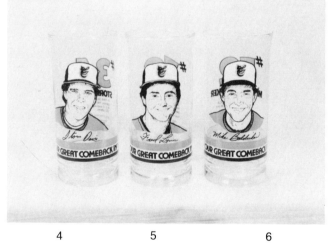

1   2   3   4   5   6

Cal Ripken Jr. – 1	1( )2
Rick Dempsey – 2	2( )2
Eddie Murray – 3	3( )2
Storm Davis – 4	4( )2
Fred Lynn – 5	5( )2
Mike Boddicker – 6	6( )2

BATMAN – Set #BAT
Sonoco Gas Promotion (1989) Canadian
4¼" Black/White and Yellow

1	2	3

Batman emblem and name . . . . 1( )2
Batman Standing emblem and name . . . . . . 2( )2
Batman Bust . . . . 3( )2

4	5	6

Batman Standing in front of car . . . . 4( )2
Batman's car and emblem . . . . 5( )2
Batman's starship . . . . 6( )2

BATTLESTAR GALACTICA – Set #BAG
(1979) Universal Studios – 5 15/16" Rd. Btm.

1	2	3	4

Apollo . . . . 1( )1
Commander Adama . . . . 2( )1

Cyclon Warriors . . . . 3( )2
Starbuck . . . . 4( )1

B.C. ICE AGE – Set #BCI
(1981) Arby's 5¼"

1	2	3	4

8

5   6

Ball and Bat	1(	)2
Listening To Shell	2(	)2
Riding On Wheel	3(	)2
Stupid Look / Man	4(	)2
Woman / Club / Snake	5(	)2
Zot	6(	)2

B.C. ICE AGE BY HART – Set #BCA
All glasses are thick and heavy base with finger
indentions in glass for holding

1   4

Zot – 3 7/16"	1(	)2
Man on Rock Wheel – 3 7/8"	2(	)2
Man on Rock Wheel in frosted sq. – 5¼"	3(	)2
Pitcher	4(	)2

BICENTENNIAL GLASSES / BICENTENARY – Set #BIC
(1776-1976) – 5½" S.S. Heavy Base in 4 color

1   2   3

4   5   6

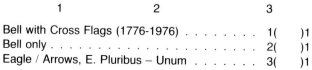

Bell with Cross Flags (1776-1976)	1(	)1	Eagle / Cannon / Sheild / 3 Flags	4(	)1
Bell only	2(	)1	Eagle / Drum / Justice / Liberty	5(	)1
Eagle / Arrows, E. Pluribus – Unum	3(	)1	Eagle / Drum / Powder Horn / Flintlock	6(	)1

9

BICENTENNIAL SERIES – Set #BIS
Burger Chef (1975) – Men of Mount Rushmore
5¼" Ind. Base

3　　　2

Jefferson, Thomas . . . . 1(　)2
Lincoln, Abraham . . . . 2(　)2
Franklin, Benjamin . . . . 3(　)2
Washington, George . . . . 4(　)2
Revere, Paul . . . . 5(　)2
Kennedy, John . . . . 6(　)2

BICENTENNIAL MISCELLANEOUS – Set #BIX
(1976)

3¼" Del. of Ind. – Liberty Bell / Eagle / Flag
　red & blue . . . . 1(　)1
3½" Del. of Ind. – Wrap Around Parchment
　brown & beige . . . . 2(　)1
5¼" Happy Birthday America – Crossed Flag, r/w/b　3(　)1
5½" Paul Revere / Midnight Ride / Old North Church　4(　)1
5⅝" Historical Patriotic Scenes – Libbey Glass Co. .　5(　)1
6⅛" Tankard – Etched Liberty Bell . . . . 6(　)1
6¾" Uncle Sam – r/w/b . . . . 7(　)1
6¾" Betsy Ross Sewing Flag – r/w/b . . . . . . 8(　)1

BIG TOP PEANUT BUTTER – Set #BTC
Children Songs

1　　　　4　　　　8

Billy Boy . . . . 1(　)1
Farmer In The Dell . . . . 2(　)1
Jack and Jill . . . . 3(　)1
London Bridge Is Falling Down . . . . 4(　)1
Mary Had A Little Lamb . . . . 5(　)1
Pop – Goes The Weasel . . . . 6(　)1
Rock-A-Bye Baby . . . . 7(　)1
Sing A Song of Sixpence . . . . 8(　)1
The Mulberry Bush . . . . 9(　)1
Three Blind Mice . . . . 10(　)1
Twinkle, Twinkle Little Star . . . . 11(　)1
What Can The Matter Be . . . . 12(　)1
Where Has My Little Dog Gone . . . . 13(　)1

BIG TOP PEANUT BUTTER – Set #BTS
(1940's - 1950's) Song Series
5⅛" Heavy Rd. Base

9   23   20   13

After The Ball	1(	)1
Auld Lang Syne	2(	)1
Bonnie	3(	)1
Camptown Races	4(	)1
Comin Through The Rye	5(	)1
Darling Clementine	6(	)1
Daisy, Daisy	7(	)1
Dixieland	8(	)1
Good Night Ladies	9(	)1
Good Bye My Lover Good Bye	10(	)1
Home Sweet Home	11(	)1
How Dry I Am	12(	)1
I've Been Wukkin' On The Railroad	13(	)1
Jeannie With The Light Brown Hair	14(	)1
Long Long Ago	15(	)1
My Old Kentucky Home	16(	)1
Oh Susanna	17(	)1
Old Folk's At Home	18(	)1
Row Row Row Your Boat	19(	)1
Silver Threads Among The Gold	20(	)1
Ta, Ra, Ra, Boum Te Ay	21(	)1
The Flying Trapeze	22(	)1
The Girl I Left Behind	23(	)1
The Eye's of Texas	24(	)1
The Band Played On	25(	)1
The Old Gray Mare	26(	)1
The Flying Trapeze	27(	)1
Turkey in the Straw	28(	)1
When You And I Were Young Maggie	29(	)1
You Tell Me Your Dream	30(	)1

BIG TOP PEANUT BUTTER – Set #BTG
State Glasses

19   24   39   45

AL	1(	)1	IA	13(	)1	NE	25(	)1	RI	37(	)1
AZ	2(	)1	KS	14(	)1	NV	26(	)1	SC	38(	)1
AR	3(	)1	KY	15(	)1	NH	27(	)1	SD	39(	)1
CA	4(	)1	LA	16(	)1	NJ	28(	)1	TN	40(	)1
CO	5(	)1	ME	17(	)1	NM	29(	)1	TX	41(	)1
CT	6(	)1	MD	18(	)1	NY	30(	)1	UT	42(	)1
DE	7(	)1	MA	19(	)1	NC	31(	)1	VT	43(	)1
FL	8(	)1	MI	20(	)1	ND	32(	)1	VA	44(	)1
GA	9(	)1	MN	21(	)1	OH	33(	)1	WA	45(	)1
ID	10(	)1	MS	22(	)1	OK	34(	)1	WV	46(	)1
IL	11(	)1	MO	23(	)1	OR	35(	)1	WI	47(	)1
IN	12(	)1	MT	24(	)1	PA	36(	)1	WY	48(	)1

JAMES BOND – Set #JBG
4" – S.O.R. Glass

1   2   3   4

For Your Eyes Only	. . . .	1( )	2
Moonraker	. . . .	2( )	2
Spy Who Love Me	. . . .	3( )	2
View To Kill	. . . .	4( )	2

BORDEN DAIRY – Set #BDC

3   4   5

9   10   11

15   16

19	20	21

Aunt Elsie – 3½" blue w/red ring & blue verse . 1( )4
Aunt Elsie – 3½" red w/red ring & red verse . . . 2( )4
Baby Beulah – 3½" black w/red ring & black verse . 3( )4
Celestine – 3½" black w/red ring & black verse . 4( )4
Little Lola – 3½" brown w/red ring & brown verse . 5( )4
Beulah – 4¾" brown outline – 7 yellow lines
   above & below . . . . 9( )3
Elmer – 4¾" brown outline – 7 yellow lines
   above & below . . . . 10( )3
Elsie – 4¾" brown outline – 7 yellow lines
   above & below . . . . 11( )3
Beau-regard in yellow. Star's around head
   Libbey 4¾" . . . . 15( )3
Beulah in yellow. Star's around head
   Libbey 4¾" . . . . 16( )3

25	27	26

Beulah / Elmer – Flag & Sport's Car
   Federal 4¾" pink . . . . 19( )3
Beulah / Elsie on Roller Skates – 4¾" Fed. green . 20( )3
Elsie / Beau-regard Tugging on Rope
   4¾" lt. blue Fed. . . . . 21( )3
Borden Bicentennial – Playing Drums & Flute
   hvy base . . . . 25( )3
Elmer Firing Gun – 3 7/16" S.O.R. Glass
   red / white w/ brown outline . . . . 26( )3
Elsie Holding Flowers – Swedish Scene
   in yellow 4¾" . . . . 27( )3
Elsie (1940's) Soda Fountain Type 6¼" . . . . . 28( )3
Elsie in yellow sunflower 5 9/16" S.S., hvy base . 29( )3

BOSSIE THE COW – Set #BTC
(1930's) 4½" Thin S.S. Slight Flare at Rim

1	2	3

Bossie Studies Hard In School – red . . . . . . 1( )4
Most Cow's Don't Like To Be Alone – purple . . 2( )4
The Minute Bossie Graduated – green . . . . . 3( )4

BOSTON RED SOXS – Set #BRS
Papa Gino's (1976) – 6⅛"

Bill Lee . . . . 1( )3	Louis Tiant . . . . 3( )3
Fred Lynn . . . . 2( )3	Rico Petrocelli . . . . 4( )3

BOZO THE CLOWN AND HIS BUDDIES – Set #BZC
(1965) 5¼" Capitol Records Inc.

Belinda . . . . 1( )2
Butchy . . . . 2( )2
Elvis . . . . 3( )2
Mr. Lion . . . . 4( )2
Professor Tweedysoofer . . . . 5( )2

BZC 1   BZX 2

BOZO THE CLOWN MISCELLANEOUS – Set #BZX

Bozo The Clown and Friends in white outline 5⅝". 1( )2
Bozo and His Buddies – Larry Harmon Pict. (1965) . 2( )2
Bozo in blue, red, yellow – Shown in different poses
(1965) 5½" – Jelly Glass . . . . 3( )2

1

BROCKWAY GLASS CO. – Set #BRO
Anniversary and Grand Openings

3   5   4

Brockway Glass Co. symbol of quality . . . . . . 1( )1
Brockway 50th Anniversary 4⅝" (1907-1957)
　　Muskogee, OK . . . . 2( )1
Brockway Open House, Lapel, IN (9-24-53)
　　dark green print . . . . 3( )1

Brockway Symbol Glass 4⅝", thin,
　　girl / dog on reverse . . . . 4( )1
Brockway Open House 25th Anniversary, Lapel, IN . 5( )1
Brockway Glass Co., Open House
　　Zanesville, OH (July 1976) . . . . 6( )1

Burger Chef – Set #BUC
(1977) 6⅛" S.S. – Creased Btm.

　　　　1　　　　　　3　　　　　　2

Burger Chef and Jeff Go Trail Riding . . . . . . 1( )5
Burgerini's Rabbit Hops Away . . . . 2( )5
Burgorilla Falling Head Over Heels . . . . 3( )5

　　　　6　　　　　　5　　　　　　4

Fangburger Gets A Scare . . . . 4( )5
Frankenburger Scores A T.D. . . . . 5( )5
Werewolf Goes Skate Boarding . . . . 6( )5

BURGER KING – Set #BUK
(1776-1976) 5½" Heavy Ped. Base

Crossed Flags . . . . 1( )1
Eagle & Shield . . . . 2( )1

Liberty Bell . . . . 3( )1
Patriots playing instruments . . . . 4( )1

BURGER KING – Set #BUR
(1978) Brockway Glass 6 5/16"

　　　　3　　　　　　　　1

I'll Turn Onions Into Rings (onion rings) . . . . . 1( )3
I've Got the Magic That It Takes (shakes) . . . . 2( )3
It Isn't Luck – It Isn't Chance (fries) . . . . 3( )3
See These Burgers, Watch Them Spin (burgers) . 4( )3

BURGER KING – Set #BKG
(1979) 5 15/16" Rd. Btm.

1

2

3

4

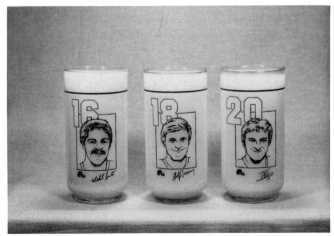

Burger King . . . . 1( )1
Burger Thing . . . . 2( )1
Duke of Doubt . . . . 3( )1
Shake A Lot . . . . 4( )1
Wizard of Fries . . . . 5( )1

5

CANADIAN HOCKEY PLAYERS – Set #CHP
(1979) A & W Root Beer

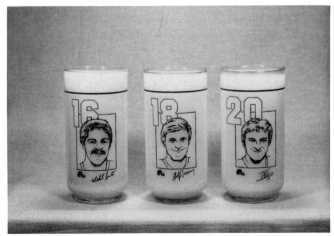

1   2   3
Michel Goulet #16 . . . . 1( )3
Marian Stastny #18 . . . . 2( )3
Anton Stastny #20 . . . . 3( )3

AL CAPP – Set #ALC
(1949) 4¾" Federal Glass Co.

| 1-9 | 2-10 | 3-11 | 4-12 | | | 5-13 | 6-14 | 7-15 | 8-16 |

		4¾"	5¼"
Daisy Mae	1( )3	9( )3
Li'l Abner	2( )3	10( )3
Lonesome Polecat	3( )3	11( )3
Mammy Yocum	4( )3	12( )3

Marryin' Sam	5( )3	13( )3
Pappy Yocum	6( )3	14( )3
Shmoos	7( )3	15( )3
Unwashable Jones	8( )3	16( )3

AL CAPP – Set #ACG
(1975) Brockway Glass Co. – Sneaky Petes in Alabama
6 5/16"

1   2   3   4

Daisy Mae	1(	)5
Joe Btsfplk	2(	)6
Li'l Abner	3(	)5
Mammy Yocum	4(	)5
Pappy Yocum	5(	)5
Sadie Hawkins	6(	)5

5   6

AL CAPP – Set #ACS
(1975) Sneaky Pete's Rest. – ¾" ind. base

Li'l Abner	1( )6	Daisy Mae	4( )6
Joe Btsptflk	2( )6	Mammy Yocum	5( )6
Sadie Hawkins	3( )6	Pappy Yocum	6( )6

CARE BEARS – Set #CRB
(1983) Pizza Hut – Libbey Glass Co. 6"

1   3   5   6

Cheer Bear / Enjoy . . . . 1( )1
Friend – Friend's Bring Fun . . . . 2( )2
Funshine Bear / Feeling Funtastic . . . . 3( )1
Good Luck Bear / mint in color . . . . 4( )2
Grumpy Bear / Hugs Welcome . . . . 5( )1
Tenderheart Bear / Share Some Love . . . . . . 6( )1

CARE BEARS – Set #CAB
(1984) Similar to Pizza Hut – American Greetings Corp.
round bottom, slight design difference

Bedtime Bear . . . . 1( )2	Funshine Bear . . . . 2( )2

CARE BEARS – Set #CBC
Libbey Glass Co. – Those Characters From Cleveland
Indented base

4

	1985 A.G. 5 1/16"	1986 5 1/16"
Bedtime Bear	1( )2	13( )2
Cheer Bear	2( )2	14( )2
Good Luck Bear	3( )2	15( )2
Share Bear	4( )2	16( )2

HOPALONG CASSIDY – Set #CAH
5" slight flare top – milk glass, Hopalong on front
of glass and verse on back

1   4   3   1

Breakfast – Hoppy Twirling Larrot . . . . 1( )5	Snack – Hoppy Behind Broken Wagon Wheel . . 3( )8
Lunch . . . . 2( )5	Dinner – Ready To Draw Guns . . . . 4( )5

CHARMER'S BY HALLMARK – Set #CRM
(1975) 5 1/16" slight flare at top

It's Good To Take Time . . . . 1( )2
Thankfulness Grows . . . . 2( )2
Try Your Best . . . . 3( )2
When There's Love In The Home . . . . 4( )2

4

CHARMER'S BY HALLMARK – Set #CHA
(1976) 6½" Glass Set

A Dream Is A Door To Tomorrow . . . . 1( )3

1

THE CHIPMUNKS – Set #CPM
(1985) Bagdesarian Productions – Libbey Glass Co.
6" rd. btm.

1   4   2   3

Alvin	1(	)1
Simon	2(	)1
Theodore	3(	)1
Chipettes – Karman / Ross Prod.	4(	)1

CHRISTMAS GLASSES – Set #CHR
Small barrel type / red with green verse 5 1/16"

1-9   2-10   5-13   8-16

3-11   4-12   6-14   7-15

	4¼"		5⅛"	
Santa in sleigh going over house top	1(	)0	9(	)0
Children in front of fire place . .	2(	)0	10(	)0
Santa's face / his cheeks were like roses	3(	)0	11(	)0

Santa in front of fire place . . .	4(	)0	12(	)0
Santa in sleigh over house & church	5(	)0	13(	)0
Mouse in bed	6(	)0	14(	)0
Ma and Pa in bed	7(	)0	15(	)0
Children in bed	8(	)0	16(	)0

CINCINNATI BENGALS NFL – Set #CIB
Burger Chef Helment (1979) 5⅝" smoked

Cincinnati Bengals	1(	)1	Philadelphia Eagles	5(	)1
Cleveland Browns	2(	)1	Pittsburgh Steelers	6(	)1
Green Bay Packers	3(	)1	Seattle Seahawks	7(	)1
New York Giants	4(	)1	Washington Redskins	8(	)1

CINCINNATI REDS MLB – Set #CIR
King Kwik in blue – 6¼" Red Bands

1	2	3			4	5	6	
Bench . . . . 1( )4					Griffey . . . . 4( )4			
Conception . . . . 2( )4					Morgan . . . . 5( )4			
Foster . . . . 3( )4					Rose . . . . 6( )4			

CLEVELAND BROWNS – Set #CLB
Wendy's (1981) 6¼"

Brian Sipe	1( )2
Doug Dieken	2( )2
Lyle Alzado	3( )2
Mike Pruitt	4( )2

3   2   4   1

COCA COLA SHAKER – Set #CCS
Coca Cola in red, glass stain with green border
above and below

6½" Stem	1( )2
3⅛" S.O.R.	2( )2
7⅞" Shaker with pour spout	3( )2

1   3

COCA COLA CALENDAR GIRLS – Set #CGC
Centennial Collection 4⅛" high – Lead Crystal
square base

1916	1( )3
1924	2( )3
1925	3( )3

COCA COLA CALENDAR GIRLS – Set #CGF
Tiara Glass Co. – 6" soda glass, frosted picture

1	2	3	4

1909	1( )3
1927	2( )3
1944	3( )3
1954	4( )3

CLASSIC COLLECTION – Set #CCC
from Libbey Glass Co. 5¼"

Mobie Dick	1( )3
Robin Hood	2( )3
Three Musketeers	3( )3
Treasurer Island	4( )3

CLASSIC COLLECTION – Set #CCC
from Libbey Glass Co. 5¼"

5-9   6-10   7-11   8-12

	3¼" W.M.		5¼"	
Alice in Wonderland	5(	)3	9(	)3
Gulliver's Travels	6(	)3	10(	)3
Tom Sawyer	7(	)3	11(	)3
Wizard of Oz	8(	)3	12(	)3

COCA COLA MLB SPORTS – Set #CMS
Libbey Glass Co. 6" ind. base, S.S.

1   3   4

Johnny Bench	1(	)6
Pete Rose	2(	)6
Tom Seavers	3(	)6
Carl Yastrzemski	4(	)6

MAGNIFICENT LADIES FROM COCA COLA – Set #CML
Libbey Glass Co. 5½" flare top

1   2   3   4

5   6

96771 1 of 6 series I	1(	)2
96772 2 of 6 series I	2(	)2
96773 3 of 6 series I	3(	)2
96774 4 of 6 series I	4(	)2
96775 5 of 6 series I	5(	)2
96776 6 of 6 series I	6(	)2

McCROY STORES INC. – Set #CMC
Christmas glasses – different heights and shapes

1   4   5   3   6

(1982) 100th Anniversary	1(	)1
(1984) Santa & Sleigh / Toy Shoppe		
beside sleigh	2(	)1
Rudolph watching santa fly by	3(	)1
Santa & reindeer and elves in front		
of North Pole	4(	)1
Santa & reindeer flying over house	5(	)1
Sleigh loaded with gifts	6(	)1

SANTA – Set #CSC
Coca Cola Christmas 6" rd. btm.

1   2   3

4   5   6

Santa/finger to mouth 93751 1 of 3 series I . . .	1(	)0	Santa/"Wherever I Go", 93761 1 of 3 series II . .	4(	)0
Santa/elves 93751 2 of 3 series I	2(	)0	Santa/legs crossed 93761 2 of 3 series II . . .	5(	)0
Santa/old man 93751 3 of 3 series I	3(	)0	Santa/bag of toys 93761 3 of 3 series II	6(	)0

COCA COLA MISCELLANEOUS – Set #CCX

3   5

7

9

11

79   89   13

15

17 Front

17 Back

19

21

37   39   87

47

49

57 Front

91

57 Back

31

81

33

27

99

55

77

25

67

83

51

45

85

63

35

29

41

Tray Girl . . . . 1( )2
11th Annual Conv. – flare glass Dallas, TX (1985)
 two cowboys and one girl . . . . 3( )1
11th Annual Conv. – flare glass Dallas, TX (1985)
 cowboy hat off . . . . 5( )1
75th Anniversary Dallas – soda glass . . . . . 7( )1
100th Centennial Celebration – soda glass . . . 9( )1
Autumn Look 5½" ind. base . . . . 11( )0
Bresler's 33 Flavors . . . . 13( )1
Calendar Girl (1913) scene red rose in hat . . . 15( )2
Carl's Jr. – 40th Anniversary (1981)
 Flare top brown & beige . . . . 17( )1
Casa Ol'e Mexican Rest. rd. btm. . . . . . . 19( )1
Clancy's (1985) 20th Anniversary rd. btm. . . . 21( )1
Cola Clan Convention Texas (set of 4) . . . . 23( )2
Coca Cola in multi. lang. all over glass
 5⅜" x 2 3/16" . . . . 25( )1
Coca Cola in white set in blk. tiffany look red border . 27( )0
Coca Cola 5 lang. in gold – USA 1976 Olympic . 29( )2
Coca Cola in white
 enjoy above stain glass look gn . . . . 31( )0
Coca Cola in white/red/green frosted rd. btm. . . 33( )0
Coca Cola white christmas trees / family 6" flare top . 35( )1

Drink Coca Cola around top in tiffany
 heavy base 5 9/16" . . . . 37( )1
Tome Coca Cola around top in tiffany
 heavy base 5 9/16" . . . . 39( )5
Ghostbuster's II 5½" heavy base S.S. . . . . . 41( )1
Girl Dancing – Coca Cola flare top . . . . . . 43( )1
Green Holly – Coca Cola white script
 6" flare top . . . . 45( )1
Happy Chef (1981) brown . . . . 47( )1
Jack In The Box 5½" ind. btm. – Tiffany . . . . 49( )0
Jolly Roger, Hawaii, orange color ship . . . . . 51( )2
K-Mart 20th Anniversary (1982) flare top . . . . 53( )1
Kroger 100th (1883-1983) Coca Cola flare top . 55( )1
Mothers Pizza – Girl Holding Glass (Coca Cola
 flare top . . . . 57( )1
Taco Mayo Mousecat . . . . 59( )2
Pope's Cafeterias 50th – flare top . . . . . . 61( )1
North Texas Coke Glass
 4 11/16" S.O.R. Glass . . . . 63( )1
San Antonio CCBC Opening (Sept. 1965) . . . 65( )1
Soda glass, 4 languages and english . . . . . 67( )0
SMU Mustangs, Coke Soda Glass
 5 languages, 83 Cotton Bowl . . . . 69( )1
Steak n Shake – b/w checkered cloth . . . . . 71( )1
Tab – large crease in middle of glass . . . . . 73( )0
Taco Mayo outdoor scenes Coca Cola set of 6 . 75( )1
The Archieves C.C. 16 oz. flare – recreation . . 77( )1
The Portsmouth Area is for Everyone . . . . . 79( )1
Tiffany Look, red & green, flare top . . . . . . 81( )0
Tsukuba Expo 85 – Japan Coke Soda Glass . . 83( )1
Seasons Greetings, hollie leaves top,
 coke in red btm. . . . . 85( )1
Whataburger, Cowboy, green handle
 soda glass . . . . 87( )1
Whataburger, flare top, creased btm.,
 Poinsetta on back . . . . 89( )1
Whataburger, Yellow Rose, flare glass . . . . 91( )1
Whataburger, Green Cowboy Pitcher . . . . . 93( )3
World Wide Arts, Boy and Girl on Bench . . . . 95( )1
World's Fair Knoxville, TN coke flare (1982) . . . 97( )0
(1776) Big Blue behind green pictures,
 Coke & Herfy's . . . . 99( )1

COLLEGIATE CREST – Set #COL
Coca Cola

31   1   47   42

Abilene Christian University (1906-1982) . . . . 1( )2
Arkansas State . . . . 2( )2
BC (Bakerfield College, California) . . . . 3( )2
Baker University . . . . 4( )2
Ball State University, "Noyer" Halls . . . . . . 5( )2
Bradley University Braves . . . . 6( )2
Cal Poly Mustangs, California . . . . 7( )2
Cal State University of Fullerton . . . . 8( )2
Cal State University, Fresno . . . . 9( )2
Cal State University, Longbeach . . . . 10( )2
Cal State, L.A. . . . . 11( )2
Carolina University, Greenville, NC . . . . . . 12( )2
Central Missouri State . . . . 13( )2
Clemson University, S.C. . . . . 14( )2
College of San Mateo, California . . . . 15( )2
Concordia College . . . . 16( )2

Dartmouth College	17(	)2	UCLA	34(	)2
Dickinson College	18(	)2	University of Alabama	35(	)2
East Carolina University	19(	)2	University of Georgia	36(	)2
East Michigan University	20(	)2	University of Nebraska	37(	)2
Elizabethtown	21(	)2	University of New Hampshire	38(	)2
Georgia State University	22(	)2	University of New Mexico	39(	)2
Indiana University (Southeast)	23(	)2	University of Pittsburg	40(	)2
Loyola College, Maryland	25(	)2	University of Southern California (USC)	41(	)2
Middle Tennessee State University	26(	)2	University of Texas at Arlington	42(	)2
MSU	27(	)2	University of Wisconsin/Oshkosh	43(	)2
North Texas State	28(	)2	University of Wisconsin/Milwaukee	44(	)2
Ohio State University	29(	)2	Vanderbilt	45(	)2
Pennsylvania State University	30(	)2	Wake Forest, Coca Cola	46(	)2
Plano Wildcats, Texas State AAAA (1977)	31(	)2	Washington University St. Louis 1853	47(	)2
State University N.Y. Canton	32(	)2	Wichita State University	48(	)2
Trinity University at San Antonio, Texas	33(	)2	Widener College	49(	)2

COLORADO CENTENNIAL – Set #COC
(1959) Carter Oil Co. – Frosted 6 9/16"

Arrival of the First Passenger "Train in Denver"	1(	)2
The Battle of La Glorieta Pass	2(	)2
Cattle Drive Up Texas Trail	3(	)2
Kit Carson Discussing Treaty with Ute Indian	4(	)2
Discovery of God at Little Dry Creek	5(	)2
Opera House at Central City	6(	)2

COUNTRY TIME LEMONADE – Set #CTL
(Saturday Evening Post) 5⅞" sloped indented base

1   3   4 – 5

Grandpa's Girl (2-3-1923)	1(	)1
Low and Outside (8-5-1916)	2(	)1
The Big Moment (1-25-1936)	3(	)1
The Rocking Horse (12-16-1933) red rocker	4(	)1
The Rocking Horse (12-16-1933) pink rocker	5(	)1

CURRIER AND IVES – Set #CUI
Arby's Museum of the City of N.Y.
4⅝" heavy base S.O.R.

1   2   4

American Homestead Winter . . . . 1( )1
Christmas Snow . . . . 2( )1
The Sleigh Race . . . . 3( )1
Winter In The Country / Getting Ice . . . . 4( )1

CURRIER AND IVES – Set #CUR
Arby's 4 11/16" S.O.R. Heavy Base

1-5   2-6   3-7   4-8

	1978	1981
The Road In Winter 1 of 4 . . . 1( )0	5( )0
Winter Pastime 2 of 4 . . . . . 2( )0	6( )0
American Farm in Winter 3 of 4 . 3( )0	7( )0
Frozen Up 4 of 4 . . . . 4( )0	8( )0

DAIRY QUEEN SERIES – Set #DAQ
(1976)

1   2   3   4

Young Man and Lady with Ice Cream Cones . . 1( )1
Young Man and Lady on Rail Car . . . . 2( )1
Young Man and Lady on Horse . . . . 3( )1
Young Lady on a Swing . . . . 4( )1

DAIRY QUEEN MISCELLANEOUS – Set #DQX

2   3

Little Dutch Girl Bent Over To Tap Logo . . . . . 1( )1
Santa Clause in white and black 6¼" . . . . . . 2( )1
Santa Glass, tall, black/white/red, 7½" x 2 7/16" . 3( )1
Banana Split, stained glass look . . . . 4( )1
Short ped. base with DQ Logo . . . . 5( )1

DALLAS COWBOY'S BURGER KING – Set #DAL
By Dr. Pepper 5⅝" – S.S. Ind. Base

1   2   3   4

5   6   7   8

9   10   11   12

Billy Joe Dupree . . . . 1( )1
Bob Breunig . . . . 2( )1
Charlie Waters . . . . 3( )1
Cliff Harris . . . . 4( )1
D.D. Lewis . . . . 5( )1
Drew Pearson . . . . 6( )1
Efren Herrera . . . . 7( )1
Golden Richards . . . . 8( )1
Harvey Martin . . . . 9( )1
Pat Donovan . . . . 10( )1
Randy White . . . . 11( )1
Robert Newhouse . . . . 12( )1

DENNIS THE MENACE – Set #DTM
S.S. 5½" Heavy Base, Frosted, No Logo

1 2 3

That Settle's It – Your Going To Be An Only Child . 1(   )4
This Is My Mother . . . . 2(   )4
Would You Mind Telling My Little Boy . . . . . . 3(   )4

DENVER BRONCOS – Set #DBB
Burger King (1977) 5⅝"

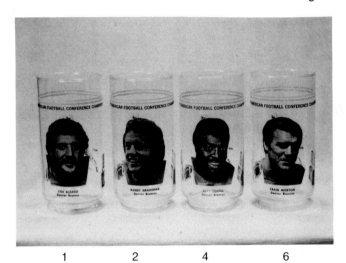

1 2 4 6

Alzado, Lyle . . . . 1(   )2
Gradeshar, Randy . . . . 2(   )2
Jackson, Tom . . . . 3(   )2
Morton, Craig . . . . 4(   )2
Moses, Haven . . . . 5(   )2
Odoms, Riley . . . . 6(   )2

DENVER BRONCOS ALL TIME GREATS – Set #DBP
KCNC (1984) Pizza Hut

1 of 4 Odoms / Wright . . . . 1(   )1
2 of 4 Johnson / Taylor . . . . 2(   )2
3 of 4 Van Heusen / Morton . . . . 3(   )2
4 of 4 Watson / Tripucka . . . . 4(   )2

DENVER BRONCOS – Set #DBA
25th Anniversary – KCNC – Pizza Hut
4⅛" S.O.R. Glass

Glassic/Watson/Tripucka/
  Alzado/Jackson/Gonsoulin . . . . 1(   )2
Heusen/Morton/Upchurch/
  Thompson/Bryon/Moses . . . . 2(   )2
Johnson/Taylor/Jackson/
  Swenson/Minor/Little . . . . 3(   )2
Odoms/Wright/Smith/Gradishar/
  Turner/Chavous . . . . 4(   )2

DETROIT TIGERS – Set #DTA
Arn't You Hungry Series 6" – Burger King (1982)
Flare top, indented base

6   2   3   4   5

Angles/Red Soxs . . . . 1( )2
Blue Jays/Yankees . . . . 2( )2
Indians/Orioles . . . . 3( )2
Royals/White Soxs . . . . 4( )2
Twins/Brewers . . . . 5( )2
Texas/Rangers/Bat . . . . 6( )2

DETROIT TIGERS – Set #DET
Sanders in white around top in orange bands

Mark Fydrich . . . . 1( )2
Ben Oglivie . . . . 2( )2
Rusty Staub . . . . 3( )2

DETROIT TIGERS – Set #DRW
Little Ceasar's (1984)

1   2   3   4

Hernandez/Lemon/Wilcox . . . . 1( )3
Lopez/Gibson/Morris . . . . 2( )3
Rozema/Trammell/Johnson . . . . 3( )3
Whitaker/Petry/Parrish . . . . 4( )3

DETROIT TIGERS – Set #DTR
Burger King (1988) 6" round bottom

1   2   3   4

At Bat . . . . 1( )2
Catching Fly Ball . . . . 2( )2
Holding Scoreboard . . . . 3( )2
Waving Pennant in Stadium . . . . 4( )2

WALT DISNEY

ALICE IN WONDERLAND – Set #WDAW
Walt Disney 4¾" – Medium weight tapered glass

3

1 Alice	1(	)7
2 Alice and Eaglet	2(	)7
3 Alice and Tweedle Dum and Dee	3(	)7
4 Walrus and Carpenter	4(	)7
5 Alice and Haughty Caterpillar	5(	)7
6 Alice and Cheshire Cat	6(	)7
7 Mad Hatter and March Hare	7(	)7
8 Queen of Hearts and Rabbit	8(	)7

ALL STAR PARADE – Set #WDAS
Walt Disney (1939)

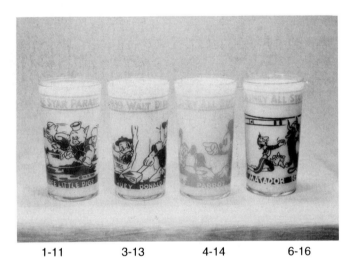

1-11   3-13   4-14   6-16

7-17   8-18   9-19   30

	No Banner 4¼"	4¼"	4 3/16"
Big Bad Wolf and the 3 Little Pigs	21( )5	1( )6	11( )5
Goofy and Wilbur	22( )5	2( )6	12( )5
Huey, Donald Duck, Dewey, Donna, Louie	23( )5	3( )6	13( )5
Minnie, Pluto, Parrot, Mickey	24( )5	4( )6	14( )5
Raccoon, Turtle, Fawn, Rabbit	25( )5	5( )6	15( )5

Senorita, Matador, Ferdinand	26( )5	6( )6	16( )5
Snow White and the Seven Dwarfs	27( )5	7( )6	17( )5
The Ugly Duckling	28( )5	8( )6	18( )5
The Greedy Pig and Colt .	29( )5	9( )6	19( )5
Wally Wal, Penguins – Polly, Baby, Peter . . .	30( )5	10( )6	20( )5

BIG RED – Set #WDBR
(Canadian) Walt Disney

Number 1	1(	)2
Number 2	2(	)2
Number 3	3(	)2
Number 4	4(	)2
Number 5	5(	)2
Number 6	6(	)2

BOSCO GLASS – Set #WDBO
Walt Disney Characters

6   1

Donald Duck	1(	)5
Clarabelle	2(	)5
Funny Bunny	3(	)5
Goof	4(	)5
Horace	5(	)5
Mickey	6(	)5
Minnie	7(	)5
Pluto	8(	)5

CANADIAN MOVIE SET – Set #WDCM
Walt Disney

Fantasia	1(	)3
Pinocchio	2(	)3
Snow White	3(	)3
Peter Pan	4(	)3

CINDERELLA – Set #WDCR
Libbey Glass Co., Walt Disney

1-9-17

2-10-18

3-11-19

4-12-20

5-13-21

6-14-22

7-15-23

8-16-24

	4¼"	4⅝"	5¼"				
Cinderella/Dog no. 1	1( )3	9( )3	17( )4	Cinderella/Coach and Horses No. 5	5( )3	13( )3	21( )4
Cinderella/Sisters No. 2 . .	2( )3	10( )3	18( )4	Cinderella/Prince No. 6 . . .	6( )3	14( )3	22( )4
Cinderella/Fairy Godmother No. 3	3( )3	11( )3	19( )4	Cinderella/Clock No. 7 . . .	7( )3	15( )3	23( )4
Cinderella/Magic Wand No. 4	4( )3	12( )3	20( )4	Cinderella/Mice/ Slipper No. 8	8( )3	16( )3	24( )4

DAVY CROCKET – Set #WDDCA
Walt Disney – 4¼" medium weight glass 2⅜"
Color Picture

1-2-3

4-5-6

7-8-9

10-11-12

13-14-15

Price Code 3

	Blue	Orange	Pink
Davy Fought War	1( )	2( )	3( )
Davy Had A Creed	4( )	5( )	6( )
O'l Grumpy Bear	7( )	8( )	9( )

	Green	White	Yellow
Davy a Happy Boy	10( )	11( )	12( )
Steady Nerves	13( )	14( )	15( )
Davy Met Indian	16( )	17( )	18( )

DAVY CROCKETT – Set #WDDCB
Walt Disney – 5 1/16" Med. Weight Glass
Slight bow in glass from top to bottom   2 11/16" M.O.

1

2

3

4

D.C. 1786-1836 – green skin btm. – Canoe/Horse . 1( )2

D.C. 1786-1836 Indian Fighter – Hero of Alamo
    red – The Alamo . . . . 2( )2

D.C. 1786-1836 Indian Fighter – Hero of Alamo
    blue – Indian Peace Pipe . . . . 3( )2

D.C. 1786-1836 Indian Fighter – Hero of Alamo
    orange canoe – Canoe Chasing Indians . . . 4( )2

DAVY CROCKETT – Set #WDDCC
5⅝" weight – rib's inside glass
3" M.O. (⅝" rim at top)

D.C. 1786-1836 Indian Fighter – Hero of Alamo
    orange Canoe Chasing Indians . . . . 1( )2

D.C. 1786-1836 Indian Fighter – Hero of Alamo
    green Fighting Bear . . . . 2( )2

DAVY CROCKETT – Set #WDDCD
5⅝" med. weight – rib's inside glass
3" M.O. (no rim at top)

D.C. 1786-1836 Indian Fighter – Hero of Alamo
    orange, Canoe Chasing Indians . . . . 1( )2

D.C. 1786-1836 Indian Fighter – Hero of Alamo
    lime outline, yellow scene – Alamo . . . . . . 2( )2

D.C. 1786-1836 Indian Fighter – Hero of Alamo
    green outline, Fighting Indian in white . . . . . 3( )2

D.C. 1786-1836 Indian Fighter – Hero of Alamo, Davy in
    Washington – green outline – white scene . . 4( )2

DAVY CROCKETT – Set #WDDCE
Walt Disney 5" Heavy Base 2½" M.O.

D.C. 1786-1836 Indian Fighter – Hero of Alamo
    blue, Indian Peace Pipe . . . . 1( )2

D.C. 1786-1836 Indian Fighter – Hero of Alamo
    orange, Canoe Chasing Indians . . . . 2( )2

D.C. 1786-1836 Indian Fighter – Hero of Alamo
    red, Davy Fighting Soldier in Alamo . . . . . . 3( )2

1

DAVY CROCKETT MISCELLANEOUS – Set #WDDX
Walt Disney – shown are height and
mouth opening (M.O.)

1   13   19   23

27   41

3 11/16" – 2" M.O. yellow & brown top half, green btm.
Chasing Indian on Horse . . . . 1( )2

4⅛" – 2" M.O. red top half – green btm.
Fighting Indian . . . . 3( )2

4½" – 2½" M.O. – red top, brown btm. – spined . 5( )2

4 11/16" – 2½" M.O. red, black – D.C. In A Jam . 7( )2

4¾" – 2⅝" M.O. brown, black,
GN-Kneeling to Shoot . . . . 9( )2

4¾" – 2⅜" M.O. red scene, green btm.
Davy Fighting Indian . . . . 11( )2

4¾" – 2¼" M.O. red scene, black btm. fluted
Davy Fighting Indian . . . . 13( )2

4¾" – 2½" M.O. lt. blue & white scene – orange skin
Davy Fighting Bear – slight bow . . . . 15( )2

4¾" – 2¾" M.O. frosted – Davy on Horse –
Farmers Dairy Milk Ice Cream . . . . 17( )2

4¾" – 2 11/16" M.O. Fed. Glass – yellow/orange
Remember the Alamo . . . . 19( )2

4¾" – 2 11/16" M.O. Fed. Glass – greenish/yellow
Davy the Hunter . . . . 21( )2

4⅝" – 2¼" M.O. red scene, yellow btm.
Davy Fighting Indian . . . . 23( )2

4⅝" – 2 3/16" M.O. Fed. Glass, brownish/yellow –
D.C. on Horse Carrying Gun . . . . 25( )2

4⅞" – 2¼" M.O. double hump btm., white –
Davy/Canoe . . . . 27( )2

5⅝" – straight sides, top half white, Fighting Alamo . 29( )2

5⅞" – top half brown, btm. half spined –
2 15/16" M.O. . . . . 31( )2

5 9/16" – ⅝" rim, top half red – Davy Fighting Indian . 33( )2

5" – 2 11/16" M.O. frosted glass,
1955 Scenes in brown . . . . 37( )2

5" – 2½" M.O. – brown/white scene, red btm. hvy. base
The Alamo Burning . . . . 39( )2

7" – 2½" M.O. – Holiday Freeze –
Davy Chasing Indians . . . . 41( )2

DISNEYLAND – Set #WDDJ
Juice Set (1950's)

Donald In Adventureland . . . . 1( )2
Goofy In Tomorrowland . . . . 2( )2
Mickey In Frontierland . . . . 3( )2
Tinker Bell In Fantasyland . . . . 4( )2

DISNEYLAND SERIES – Set #WDDS
Coca Cola – Walt Disney 5⅛"
Federal Glass Co.

	5	6	2			4	8	3
Daisy	. . . . 1( )4				Mickey	. . . . 5( )4		
Donald	. . . . 2( )4				Minnie	. . . . 6( )4		
Dumbo	. . . . 3( )4				Pinocchio	. . . . 7( )4		
Goofy	. . . . 4( )4				Pluto	. . . . 8( )4		

DONALD DUCK – Set #WDDD
Walt Disney (1930's)
Banner Top 4 13/16"

Donald Cooking – Nephews on back . . . . . . 1( )7
Donald Duck is Very Gay as His Guitar He's Playing . 2( )7
Three Little Duck's in Scout Troup . . . . 3( )7
Donald/Bicycle/Delivering Mail – orange/blue border . 4( )7
Donald Playing Golf – green/red border . . . . . 5( )7
Donald and Goofy Pushing Sleight –
    blue/yellow border . . . . 6( )7

3   1   2

DOUBLE CHARACTER – Set #WDCB
Walt Disney (in color block)

1-5   2-6   3-7   4-8

Donald Duck – Daisy Duck –				
orange	1(	)2	5(	)2
Goofy – Pluto – yellow	2(	)2	6(	)2

Minnie Mouse – Mickey Mouse				
pink	3(	)2	7(	)2
Pinocchio – Jiminy Cricket –				
blue	4(	)2	8(	)2

DUMBO SERIES – Set #WDDG
1941 Two Color

Dumbo Flying	1(	)10 +	The Five Black Crows	4(	)10 +
Dumbo and the Stork	2(	)10 +	Timothy Mouse	5(	)10 +
The Gossipy Elephants	3(	)10 +	Casey Jr.	6(	)10 +

FERDINAND THE BULL – Set #WDFB
(1938) W.D. Ent. – Libbey Glass Co.

1-7	2-8	3-9			4-10	5-11	6-12		
Ferdinand The Bull	1(	)5	7(	)5	La Senarita	4(	)5	10(	)5
Ferdinand The Calf	2(	)5	8(	)5	Matador	5(	)5	11(	)5
Ferdinand's Mama	3(	)5	9(	)5	The Bee	6(	)5	12(	)5

JUNGLE BOOK – Set #WDJB
(Canadian) Walt Disney

Bagheera	1(	)7	King Louie	4(	)7
Baloo	2(	)7	Mowgli	5(	)7
Flunkey	3(	)7	Shere Kahn	6(	)7

LADY AND THE TRAMP – Set #WDLT
Jelly Glass 7 3/16" – Walt Disney
glass seam up the side

	1	2	3

4	5	6	7

Bull . . . . 1( )3		Peg . . . . 5( )3
Dachsie . . . . 2( )3		Toughy . . . . 6( )3
Jock . . . . 3( )3		Trusty . . . . 7( )3
Pedro . . . . 4( )3		

MICKEY'S CHRISTMAS CAROL – Set #WDCC
(1982) Coca Cola – Walt Disney 6⅛"

1	2	3

Goofy . . . . 1( )2
Mickey & Morty . . . . 2( )2
Scrooge McDuck . . . . 3( )2

MICKEY MOUSE COLLECTION – Set #WDMM
By Walt Disney – Libbey Glass Co.
5 9/16" heavy base – S.S.

Donald & Daisy – You'll Look Sweet . . . . 1( )3
Mickey & Minnie – Singing O' Sole Mio . . . . . 2( )3
Mickey & Minnie – What Do You Say . . . . . . 3( )3
Mickey & Pluto – Boy! This Is A Swell Day . . . 4( )3

1	2	3	4

MICKEY AND GOOFY – Set #WDMG
7" Walt Disney

2

Goofy/Fishing in Boat (32oz. cooler) . . . . 1(   )2
Mickey/Shotgun/Pluto (32oz. cooler) . . . . 2(   )2

MICKEY MOUSE CLUB – Set #WDMC
Walt Disney Film Strip Series
Wonderful World of Disney 5 1/16"
S.S. Ind. Base – Libbey Glass Co.

| 1 | 2 | 3 | 4 |

Donald – Chip and Dale . . . . 1(   )2   Mickey – On Skates . . . . 3(   )2
Goofy – Donald's Nephews . . . . 2(   )2   Minnie – Scolding Pluto . . . . 4(   )2

MICKEY MOUSE CLUB – Set #WDMF
Mickey and Friends – Walt Disney
Libbey Glass Co. – 5 1/16" S.S. Ind. Base

| 1 | 2 | 3 | 4 |

| Donald – Bricking Wall . . . . | 1( )2 | | Mickey – Standing and Waiving . . . . | 3( )2 |
| Goofy – Fishing . . . . | 2( )2 | | Minnie – At Bathtub . . . . | 4( )2 |

MICKEY THRU THE AGES – Set #WDMA
(1988) Walt Disney – Sunoco Gas Stations
Ottowa, Can Renditions of Mickey in the Years
5⅛" S.S. Ind. Base

| | 1 | 2 | 3 | | | 4 | 5 | 6 |

(1928) Steamboat Willie – Wheel of Ship . . . . 1( )2   (1955) The Mickey Mouse Club – Mickey marching . 4( )2
(1938) Little Tailor – red feather in hat . . . . . . 2( )2   (1983) Mickey's Christmas Carol – green top hat . 5( )2
(1940) Fantasia – magic outfit . . . . 3( )2   (1988) Contemporary Mickey – red sun glasses . 6( )2

MICKEY MOUSE – Set #WDMS
Milk Glass (1930's)
ring around top of glass

Mickey Calling Someone . . . . 1( )10+   Mickey Walking . . . . 2( )10+

PETER PAN – WDPP
(1930's) 4⅜" – Walt Disney

2

Captain	1( )8
Crocodile	2( )8
Fairies	3( )8
Mermaid	4( )8
Never Bird	5( )8
Peter	6( )8
Shadow	7( )8
Tinkerbell	8( )8

PETER PAN – Set #WDPC
Canadian – Walt Disney

Captain Hook	1( )8
John	2( )8
Mr. Smee	3( )8
Peter Pan	4( )8
Tinkerbell	5( )8
Wendy	6( )8

PINOCCHIO – Set #WDPN
(1938-40) Libbey Glass Co.

| 1-25-37 | 2-26-38 | 3-27-39 | 4-28-40 |

| 5-29-41 | 6-30-42 | 7-31-43 | 8-32-44 |

| 9-33-45 | 10-34-46 | 11-35-47 | 12-36-48 |

| 23 | 18 |

Hat Series

	4³⁄₈"	4 9/16"	4 9/16"	4³⁄₄"
Blue Fairy	1( )4	13( )6	25( )4	37( )5
Cleo the Goldfish . . .	2( )4	14( )6	26( )4	38( )5
Coachman . . .	3( )4	15( )6	27( )4	39( )5
Figaro the Cat .	4( )4	16( )6	28( )4	40( )5
Gepetto	5( )4	17( )6	29( )4	41( )5
Gideon the Cat .	6( )4	18( )6	30( )4	42( )5
Honest John . .	7( )4	19( )6	31( )4	43( )5

Jiminy Cricket . .	8( )4	20( )6	32( )4	44( )5
Lampwick	9( )4	21( )6	33( )4	45( )5
Monstro the Whale	10( )4	22( )6	34( )4	46( )5
Pinocchio	11( )4	23( )6	35( )4	47( )5
Stromboli	12( )4	24( )6	36( )4	48( )5
Figaro the Cat also Comes in yellow			49( )7	
Pinocchio Walking/Band Around Top Glass/ Character Heads			50( )8	

SINGLE DISNEY CHARACTERS – Set #WDSC
(1930's) Walt Disney
Note: All glasses may not come in all sizes

1   11   19   21   31

33   35   39   13

15   23   29   27   43

9

37   41

	3½"	4¼"	4 3/8"	4⅝"	4¾"	
1st Little Pig Playing Flute red/vertical lettering	1( )	( )	( )	( )	( )	8
2nd Little Pig	3( )	( )	( )	( )	( )	8
3rd Little Pig	5( )	( )	( )	( )	( )	8
Big Bad Wolf	7( )	( )	( )	( )	( )	8
Clarabell, red walking with bell	9( )	( )	( )	( )	( )	6
Clarabell, looking in Mirror, red	11( )	( )	( )	( )	( )	6
Donald, like he's saying "And Heres..." blue vertical letters	13( )	( )	( )	( )	( )	4
Donald Saluting, blue	15( )	( )	( )	( )	( )	4
Donald Playing Football, blue	17( )	( )	( )	( )	( )	8
Elmer Elephant, Looking Shy, blue vertical letters	19( )	( )	( )	( )	( )	8
Funny Bunny, Painting Easter Egg, blue vertical letters	21( )	( )	( )	( )	( )	8
Goof, On Knee Like He's Hitch Hiking horizontal letters	23( )	( )	( )	( )	( )	9
Goof, (1937) green, Playing Saxophone	25( )	( )	( )	( )	( )	10+
Horace, coin, black	27( )	( )	( )	( )	( )	6

45

Horace, coin, red vertical lettering .	29 (	) (	) (	) (	)5
Horace on Crate, red horizontal letters .	31 (	) (	) (	) (	)5
Mickey, Looking Surprised, black vertical letters .	33 (	) (	) (	) (	)5
Mickey, Walking, black, no letters .	35 (	) (	) (	) (	)5

Mickey, Walking, black, horizontal letters	37 (	) (	) (	) (	)5
Minnie, In Love Look black vert. letters .	39 (	) (	) (	) (	)5
Minnie with Umbrella horiz. letters, black	41 (	) (	) (	) (	)5
Pluto, Tongue Out, Running, brownish/ vert. letters . . .	43 (	) (	) (	) (	)6

SLEEPING BEAUTY – Set #WDSB
(1958) Walt Disney 4 15/16"
Heavy Base, Slight Inward Curved Base

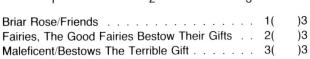

Briar Rose/Friends . . . . 1( )3
Fairies, The Good Fairies Bestow Their Gifts . . 2( )3
Maleficent/Bestows The Terrible Gift . . . . 3( )3

Prince Phillip To The Rescue . . . . 4( )3
Samson/Prince Phillip's Horse . . . . 5( )3
Sleeping Beauty Touching The Spindle . . . . . 6( )3

SNOW WHITE & SEVEN DWARFS – Set #WDSW
(1937-38) Characters Only
Libbey Glass Co.

5

7

8

11-19-27-35-43-51   14-22-30-38-46-54
    9-17-25-33-41-49   10-18-26-34-42-50

13-21-29-37-45-53   16-24-32-40-48-56
    12-20-28-36-44-52   15-23-31-47-39-55

	Bosco	4³⁄₈"	4¹⁄₂"	4⁵⁄₈"
Bashful . . .	1( )5	9( )3	17( )4	25( )5
Doc	2( )5	10( )3	18( )4	26( )5
Dopey	3( )5	11( )3	19( )4	27( )5
Grumpy . . .	4( )5	12( )3	20( )4	28( )5
Happy	5( )5	13( )3	21( )4	29( )5
Sleepy . .	6( )5	14( )3	22( )4	30( )5
Sneezy . . .	7( )5	15( )3	23( )4	31( )5
Snow White .	8( )5	16( )3	24( )4	32( )5

NOTE: Watch out for vertical and horizontal lettering

	4³⁄₄"	5 9/16"	6"
Bashful	33( )3	41( )4	49( )6
Doc	34( )3	42( )4	50( )6
Dopey	35( )3	43( )4	51( )6
Grumpy	36( )3	44( )4	52( )6
Happy	37( )3	45( )4	53( )6
Sleepy	38( )3	46( )4	54( )6
Sneezy	39( )3	47( )4	55( )6
Snow White	40( )3	48( )4	56( )6
Snow White, red, standing, with Dwarfs Heads around glass . . . . . . 57( )6			

SNOW WHITE AND THE SEVEN DWARFS – Set #WDSM
Walt Disney – Libbey Glass Co.
Music Glass Series 4³⁄₄"

1

2

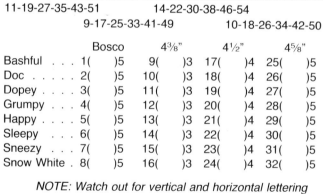

3

4

| 5 | 6 | 7 | 8 |

Bashful – Mandolin	1( )6	Happy – Cymbal	5( )6
Doc – Horn	2( )6	Sleepy – Mandolin	6( )6
Dopey – Drum	3( )6	Sneezy – Accordion	7( )6
Grumpy – Conductor	4( )6	Snow White – Singing	8( )6

THEME PARK GLASSES – Set #WDTP
Walt Disney – Thin Sides – Heavy Base

| 1-6 | 2-7 | 3-8 | 4-9 |

5-10

	4¾"	5⅝"
Donald Duck char., hvy. base . .	1( )1	6( )1
Mickey Mouse, hands behind back	2( )1	7( )1
Mickey Mouse, looking back, walking	3( )1	8( )1
Minnie Mouse, holding purse . . .	4( )1	9( )1
Pluto, ears up	5( )1	10( )1

WINNIE-THE-POOH – Set #WDWP
Sears – W.D. Productions – 5" Rd. Btm.

1

4

Tiger, Piglet, and Pooh, planting tree . . . . 1( )0
Winnie & Friends looking up at Butterfly . . . . . 2( )0
Winnie-The-Pooh and Friends, Honey Pot . . . . 3( )0
Winnie-The-Pooh for President . . . . 4( )0

WINNIE THE POOH – Set #WDPB
(1965) Canadian

Kanga and Roo . . . . 1( )3
Owl . . . . 2( )3
Pig . . . . 3( )3

Pooh . . . . 4( )3
Rabbit . . . . 5( )3
Tiger . . . . 6( )3

WALT DISNEY MISCELLANEOUS – Set #WDMX

1

7

16

19

25

28

37

39

31 + Pitcher & Box

41

America on Parade W/D, LTD Bicentennial . . .	1( )1	Mickey swayed back with arms out	28( )1
Donald Duck – 4½" green floral at btm., Donald in pink – When It's Time To Eat Your Food Remember Chocolate Milk Is Good (1950's)	4( )4	Mickey Catching Baseball – Minnie Cheerleading, 4½"	31( )1
Donald Hoeing	7( )2	Mickey and Minnie in yellow sports car, 5½" . .	33( )1
Donald On A Skate Board	13( )1	Mickey Flexing Musles, Gold Eagle Belt on 6¼"	35( )1
Happy Birthday Mickey, 50 Years of Magic W.D.P.	16( )1	Minnie Working Out with Jam Box	37( )1
Mickey on Pogo Stick	19( )1	Minnie on Skates as a Car Hop	39( )1
Mickey and Minnie Dancing (50's)	25( )1	Snow White and Dopey, juice glass & decal . . .	41( )1

DR. PEPPER MISCELLANEOUS – Set #DRX

1

11

12

13

14

20

22

25

| 34 | 36 | | 15 | 37 | 27 | 3 |

American Sampler Cross Stitch . . . . 1( )1
Be A Pepper . . . . 3( )1
Cherub's Kiss Glass . . . . 4( )0
Currier and Ives – below Dr. Pepper –
   King of Beverage . . . . 7( )1
Dr. Pepper, panel glass 5 3/16" . . . . 10( )1
Dr. Pepper 100th Anniversary
   5½" flare top/logo on back . . . . 11( )2
Dr. Pepper 100th Anniversary
   6¼" simi flare top/syrup line . . . . 12( )1
Early Day's – Old Car –
   Radio & Wright Bro., Baseball . . . . 13( )1
Flowers, yellow/white checkered
   flowers white/yellow/pink 6" flare . . . . . . 14( )1
Hollie Leaves btm. of glass, green, purple (1977) . 15( )1

Hot Air Ballon . . . . 16( )1
King of Beverages glass –
   four different scenes on glass . . . . 19( )1
King of Beverage, red/green stain glass
   white border 6⅛" . . . . 20( )1
Lady Drinking with Straw,
   stain glass window look . . . . 22( )1
Old Homes around glass, flare top . . . . 25( )1
San Antonio Fiesta (1978) . . . . 27( )1
Rainbow . . . . 28( )1
San Diego Chargers, flare coke type glass . . . 31( )1
Tiffany Look, red & gray
   Dr. Pepper King of Beverages . . . . 34( )1
Winter Scene (1978), red, green, gray . . . . . 37( )1
Wichita Falls, TX, (1882-1982) 5⅝" Ind. Base . . 36( )1

THE EMPIRE STRIKES BACK – Set #ESB
(1980) Burger King – 5⅞"

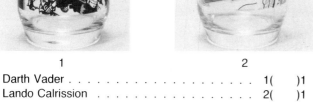

| 1 | 2 | 3 | 4 |

Darth Vader . . . . 1( )1
Lando Calrission . . . . 2( )1

Luke Skywalker . . . . 3( )1
R-2, D-2 . . . . 4( )1

ENDANGERED SPECIES – Set #ENS

Bison . . . . 1( )2
Cheetah . . . . 2( )2
Jhamin Stag . . . . 3( )2
Margay . . . . 4( )2

Marten . . . . 5( )2
Sykes Monkey . . . . 6( )2
Timber Wolf . . . . 7( )2

ENDANGERED SPECIES SERIES – Set #ENB
4 11/16" Brockway Glass Co., Rd. Btm. 12 oz.

1

2

3

4

5

7

8

Box they come in

African Elephant . . . . 1( )2		Columbia White-Tail Deer . . . . 5( )2	
Bald Eagle . . . . 2( )2		Giant Panda . . . . 6( )2	
Bengal Tiger . . . . 3( )2		Prairie Dog . . . . 7( )2	
Cape Mountain Zebra . . . . 4( )2		Whooping Crane . . . . 8( )2	

ENDANGERED SPECIES – Set #ENC
(1978) Burger Chef – 5⅝" Ind. Base
Libbey Glass Co.

1	2

Bald Eagle . . . . 1(   )1
Bengal Tiger . . . . 2(   )1

3	4

Giant Panda . . . . 3(   )1
Orangutan . . . . 4(   )1

ET – Set #ETU
(1982) Universal Studios Pizza Hut
6" Flare Top Creased Bottom

1	2

Be Good . . . . 1(   )0
Home . . . . 2(   )0

3	4

"I'll Be Right Here" . . . . 3(   )0
Phone Home . . . . 4(   )0

ET AAFES – Set #ETA
(1982) 6" Rd. Btm.

1	2	3	4

Be Good . . . . 1( )1   I'll Be Right Here . . . . 3( )1
ET Phone Home . . . . 2( )1   To The Spaceship . . . . 4( )1

FANTASY GLASSES – Set #FAN
Hazel Atlas Glass Co. – 5¾"
Medium Weight, Sloped Glass – Ice Tea Glass

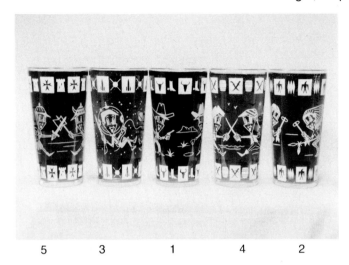

5   3   1   4   2

Cowboys – Boots and Cow, Head around top . . 1( )2
Indians – Birds and Symbols . . . . 2( )2
Spaceman – Rockets and Satelites . . . . 3( )2
Pirates – Crossed Knives and Barrels around top . 4( )2
Knights – Castle and Shield around top . . . . . 5( )2

FLINTSTONES – Set #FLT
Price Code 1 – 4 3/16" Tapered Down Body

1-2-3-4-5-6-7-8

9-10-11-12-13-14-15-16

17-18-19-20-21-22-23-24

25-26-27-28-29-30-31-32

33-34-35-36-37-38-39-40

41-42-43-44-45-46-47-48

49-50-51-52-53-54-55-56

57-58-59-60-61-62-63-64

54

| 65-66-67-68-69-70-71-72 | 73-74-75-76-77-78-79-80 | 81-82-83-84-85-86-87-88 | 89-90-91-92-93-94-95-96 |

| 97-98-99-100-101 102-103-104 | 105-106-107-108-109 110-111-112 |

(1962) 8 oz.	Red		White		Blue		Green		Orange		Pink		Aqua		Yellow	
Sports Car	1(	)1	2(	)1	3(	)1	4(	)1	5(	)1	6(	)1	7(	)1	8(	)1
Invention	9(	)1	10(	)1	11(	)1	12(	)1	13(	)1	14(	)1	15(	)1	16(	)1
Pal's at Work	17(	)1	18(	)1	19(	)1	20(	)1	21(	)1	22(	)1	23(	)1	24(	)1
Duck Pins	25(	)1	26(	)1	27(	)1	28(	)1	29(	)1	30(	)1	31(	)1	32(	)1
Having a Ball	33(	)1	34(	)1	35(	)1	36(	)1	37(	)1	38(	)1	39(	)1	40(	)1
Playing Golf	41(	)1	42(	)1	43(	)1	44(	)1	45(	)1	46(	)1	47(	)1	48(	)1
(1963) 8 oz.																
Baby Sitters	49(	)1	50(	)1	51(	)1	52(	)1	53(	)1	54(	)1	55(	)1	56(	)1
Doll Cave	57(	)1	58(	)1	59(	)1	60(	)1	61(	)1	62(	)1	63(	)1	64(	)1
(1964) 8 oz.																
Pet Show	65(	)1	66(	)1	67(	)1	68(	)1	69(	)1	70(	)1	71(	)1	72(	)1
Catching Fish	73(	)1	74(	)1	75(	)1	76(	)1	77(	)1	78(	)1	79(	)1	80(	)1
Playing Baseball	81(	)1	82(	)1	83(	)1	84(	)1	85(	)1	86(	)1	87(	)1	88(	)1
Beach	89(	)1	90(	)1	91(	)1	92(	)1	93(	)1	94(	)1	95(	)1	96(	)1
Birthday Party	97(	)1	98(	)1	99(	)1	100(	)1	101(	)1	102(	)1	103(	)1	104(	)1
Goes Hunting	105(	)1	106(	)1	107(	)1	108(	)1	109(	)1	110(	)1	111(	)1	112(	)1

Flintstones Characters under glass: Pebbles, Bamm, Bamm, Fred, Wilma, Barney, Betty, Dino
Variation/Clear Glass – No Scene – Character in Bottom . . . . 113( )1

THE FLINTSTONE KID'S – Set #FLK
(1986) 6" Hanna-Barbera – Pizza Hut
Rd. Btm.

1	2	3	4

Barney . . . . 1(　)0

Betty . . . . 2(　)0

Freddy . . . . 3(　)0

Wilma . . . . 4(　)0

FLINTSTONE – Set #FLC
(1962) Jelly Glass – Hanna-Barbera

1

All characters, black & white with Flinstones
at the top of glass in yellow 5⅛" . . . . 1(　)3
Quick Draw McGraw . . . . 3(　)3
Yogie Bear . . . . 4(　)3

GARFIELD MISCELLANEOUS – Set #GRX

5　　　　4

5" Drinking out of Coke Bottle – S.S. Goosh . . 1(　)1
5⅞" Blowing Bubbles, creased base . . . . 2(　)1
6" Whee, Riding Ice Cubes, S.S. . . . . 3(　)1
6¼" Garfield in Suit, drink in one hand
　　Garfields Cafe . . . . 4(　)3
4 9/16" Garfield in Suit, Drink in one hand
　　Garfields Cafes . . . . 5(　)3
Garfield Holding Balloons . . . . 6(　)1

GHOSTBUSTERS II – Set #GHO
Sunoco Canadian Gas Co.
5" Ind. Base

| 1 | 2 | 6 | | 4 | 5 | 3 |

Ecto – 1A . . . . 1( )2		
Nunzio Scoleri . . . . 2( )2		
Six Eyes . . . . 3( )2		

Slimmer . . . . 4( )2		
Slimmer/Driving . . . . 5( )2		
Tony Scoleri . . . . 6( )2		

THE GOONIES – Set #GOO
(1985) Warner Bros., Godfathers Pizza
5⅝" S.S. Ind. Base – Libbey Glass Co.

| 1 | 2 | 3 | 4 |

Data on the Waterslide . . . . 1( )1
Goonies in the Organ Chamber . . . . 2( )1

Sloth and the Goonies . . . . 3( )1
Sloth Comes To The Rescue . . . . 4( )1

GREEN BAY PACKERS – Set #GBP
National Football League – Pizza Hut 6¼"

Bart Star . . . . 1( )3	
Paul Hornung . . . . 2( )3	
Ray Nitschke . . . . 3( )3	
Willie Davis . . . . 4( )3	
Vince Lombard . . . . 5( )3	
Jerry Kramer . . . . 6( )3	

2   3   5   6

GUINESS BOOK OF WORLD RECORDS – Set # GBW
(1976) Sterling

1   3

2

4 1/16" Golfer/Bicycle/Baseball Player . . . . . . 1( )1
5½" Apple Peeling/Larcest Wig/Modern Dancing . 2( )1

6¾" Most Ice Cream/Longest Shower/
   Modern Dancing . . . . 3( )1

GULF COLLECTOR SERIES – Set #GCS

1-7   6-12   5-11

3-9   2-8   4-10

	S.O.R. 4"	Hvy. Base 6¼"
Old Spindletop	1( )3	7( )3
The Dawning of a New ERA . . .	2( )3	8( )3
The Great Depression Years . . .	3( )3	9( )3

The Roaring 20's	4( )3	10( )3
The World War I Years	5( )3	11( )3
World's First Drive-In Ser. Sta. Pittsburgh, PAS (1918)	6( )3	12( )3

HADACOL – Set #HAD
3 9/16" Federal Glass Co.
All have same scenes but different color

Sunday . . . . 1( )2
Monday . . . . 2( )2
Tuesday . . . . 3( )2
Wednesday . . . . 4( )2
Thursday . . . . 5( )2
Friday . . . . 6( )2
Saturday . . . . 7( )2

2

3

5

6

7

Back – 2-3-5-6-7

8

9

10

11

12

13

	Record/ on back	Blank back
Joanie	1( )10	8( )1
Potsie	2( )10	9( )1
Ralph	3( )10	10( )1
The Fonz	4( )10	11( )1
The Fonz (in office – Aronld's Restroom)	5( )10	

The Fonz (Motorcycle) . . . . 13( )3
The Fonz (Motorcycle –
Arnold's – Thumb Up) . . . . 6( )10
The Fonz (Motorcycle – Arnold's
Looking Ahead) . . . . 7( )10

ROGER HARGRAVES – Set #HAR
Indiana Glass Co.
5 13/16" Creased and Ind. Base

| | 1 | | 2 | | | 3 | | 4 |

| Little Miss Helpful | . . . . | 1( )2 | | Mr. Funny | . . . . | 3( )2 |
| Little Miss Shy | . . . . | 2( )2 | | Mr. Tickle | . . . . | 4( )2 |

ROGER HARGRAVES – Set #HGR
Indiana Glass Co.
5 13/16" Creased Base
two lines above and below character

| Mr. Blimp | . . . . | 1( )2 | | Mr. Silly | . . . . | 3( )2 |
| Little Miss Neat | . . . . | 2( )2 | | Little Miss Sunshine | . . . . | 4( )2 |

HELD, JOHN JR. – Set #HJJ
(1932) All Black Char. – Unknown Origin
5 3/16" Very Thin Glass

| | 1 | 3 | 4 | | | 5 | 6 |

Happy Days	. . . .	1( )6		To The Ladies	. . . .	4( )6
	. . . .	2( )6		Lamp Post/Two Men	. . . .	5( )6
Here's How	. . . .	3( )6		Lamp Post/Policeman	. . . .	6( )6

HERITAGE COLLECTOR SERIES – Set #HCS
(1976) from Coca Cola 5 9/16"
Spirit of 1776

1   2   3   4

Betsy Ross & Old Glory /
  Washington Crossing Delaware . . . . 1( )1
Nathan Hale/John Paul Jones . . . . 2( )1
Dec of Ind. – Paul Revere . . . . 3( )1
The Minute Men – Valley Forge . . . . 4( )1

HERITAGE COLLECTION SERIES – Set #HFB
Famous Bldgs. 5 3/16" Short ¾" Ind. Base

4

Betsy Ross House, Philadelphia, PENN . . . . . 1( )5
Independence Hall, Philadelphia, PENN . . . . . 2( )5
Jefferson Memorial, Washington, D.C. . . . . . . 3( )5
Monticello "Little Mountain" –
  Charlottesville, Virginia . . . . 4( )5
Mount Vernon – Fairfax County, Virginia . . . . 5( )5
Statue of Liberty, N.Y. Harbor . . . . 6( )5
United State Capitol, Washington, D.C. . . . . 7( )5
Washington Monument, Washington, D.C. . . . . 8( )5
Pitcher with De. of Ind. . . . . 9( )5

HERITAGE – Set #HNF
National Flag Foundation – Coca Cola
(1975-1976) Herfy's Food
Rd. Btm. 6"

4   13   15   7   3

Alamo . . . . 1( )1
Bennington . . . . 2( )1
Bunker Hill . . . . 3( )1
California Bear . . . . 4( )1
Commodore Perry . . . . 5( )1
Cowpens . . . . 6( )1
First Stars and Stripes . . . . 7( )1
General Fremont . . . . 8( )1
Grand Union . . . . 9( )1
Green Mountains . . . . 10( )1
Iwo Jima . . . . 11( )1
Promontory Point . . . . 12( )1
Rattlesnake . . . . 13( )1
Star Spangled Banner . . . . 14( )1
Taunton . . . . 15( )1
Washington's Cruisers . . . . 16( )1

1   2   3

5   9

10   11   12

13   15

17

HERITAGE – Set #HPP
Pittsburgh Press – Flag Series
6½" Heavy Base Pedestal Type Series VII

1   2   3   4

First Men on the Moon . . . . 1( )1
Bunker Hill . . . . 2( )1
Confederate Flag . . . . 3( )1
Star Spangle Banner . . . . 4( )1
Commodore Perry . . . . 5( )1
First Stars and Stripes . . . . 6( )1
Iwo Jima . . . . 7( )1
Gadsden . . . . 8( )1

HERITAGE COLLECTOR SERIES – Set #HRP
Patriots – Coca Cola 6⅛" – 1" Ind. Base Glass

1   2   3   4

George Washington Times That Try Men's Souls . 1( )1
John Paul Jones I Have Not Begun To Fight . . 2( )1

Patrick Henry Give Me Liberty or Give Me Death . 3( )1
Paul Revere The Regulars Are Out . . . . 4( )1

HOLLY HOBBIE

HOLLY HOBBIE – Set#HHBJ
Bouquet of Joy Series

Happiness is Just Being Yourself . . . . 1( )1
Let Joy Blossom in Your Heart . . . . 2( )1
Life Is Filled with Sweet Surprises . . . . . . 3( )1
Love Makes the World a Beautiful Place . . . . 4( )1
Make Everyday a Fine Bouquet . . . . 5( )1
Today Can Be The Start of Something New . . . 6( )1

HOLLY HOBBIE – Set #HHCC
Country Kitchen Series

Don't Forget To Add The Love . . . . 1( )1
Life is Simply Delicious . . . . 2( )1
Love is the Little Things You Do . . . . 3( )1
Nice Surprises are the Spice of Life . . . . . . 4( )1
Treat Yourself to a Happy Day . . . . 5( )1

HOLLY HOBBIE – Set #HHHF
and Her Friends – Coca Cola

A Little Smile Says A Lot . . . . 1( )1
Being Yourself is the Best Way To Be . . . . . 2( )1
Friends are for Thinking and Caring About . . . 3( )1

Good Friends Make the Best Company . . . . . 4( )1
Make Every Day a Sunshine Day . . . . 5( )1
Take Delight in the Little Things . . . . 6( )1

HOLLY HOBBIE – Set #HHAF
and Friends – Merry Christmas
Heavy base – Flare top 5 13/16"

3   4   5   1

Christmas is Fun for Everyone . . . . 1( )1
Christmas is here the Nicest Time of Year . . . 2( )1
Happy Ways Brighten the Holidays . . . . 3( )1
Holiday Pleasures are Lifes Sweetest Treasurers . 4( )1
Love is the Magic of Christmas . . . . 5( )1
There is a Special Glow at Christmas . . . . . . 6( )1

HOLLY HOBBIE – Set #HHHT
Happy Talk Series

1   2   3

4   5   6

A Good Example is the Best Teacher . . . . . . 1( )1
Friendship Makes Rough Roads Smooth . . . . 2( )1
Happiness Is Meant To Be Shared . . . . 3( )1
Love Is The Little Things You Do . . . . 4( )1

The Easiest Tasks are Those Done with Love . 5( )1
The Happiest Times are
    Those Shared with Friends . . . . 6( )1

HOLLY HOBBIE – Set #HHHO
Happy Holidays (1980)

1   2   3   4

Christmas Is Sharing (1980) 1 of 4 . . . . 1( )1
Wrap Each Christmas Gift In Love (1980) 2 of 4 . 2( )1
Share a Little Christmas Spirit (1980) 3 of 4 . . . 3( )1
Deck the Halls with Joy & Gladness (1980) 4 of 4 . 4( )1

HOLLY HOBBIE – Set #HHHA
Holidays (1981)

A Gift of Love Especially for You . . . . 1( )1
Christmas Puts A Song in Heart . . . . 2( )1
Dreams Can Come True . . . . 3( )1
Happiest Days . . . . 4( )1
Happy Ways Bless Christmas Days . . . . 5( )1
Holidays are Filled with Happy Sounds . . . . . 6( )1
Holidays are the Happies Times . . . . 7( )1
The Holidays Have a Magic All Their Own . . . 8( )1
Tis The Season To Be Happy . . . . 9( )1
Tis The Season For Fun . . . . 10( )1

1   8   10

HOLLY HOBBIE – Set #HHHB
Holidays (1982)

Holidays Are Meant To Be Shared – Holly/Story . 1( )1
Share in the Fun of the Season – H/R Sledding . 2( )1
Wishing You the Happiness –
    Holly/H Picking Holly . . . . 3( )1

1   2   3

HOLLY HOBBIE – Set #HHMC
Merry Christmas – No ring above and below
Holly at bottom of glass – 5⅞" ind. base

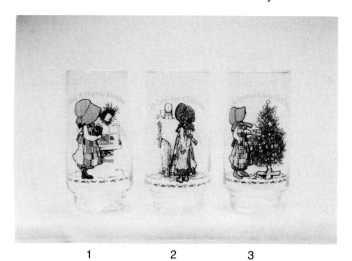

Have a Happy Holiday . . . . 1( )1
It's Time for Christmas . . . . 2( )1
There is a Special Glow at Christmas . . . . . . 3( )1

1   2   3

HOLLY HOBBIE – Set #HHMA
Merry Christmas
Ring above & below Holly at bottom

Christmas is a Gift of Joy	1(	)1
Christmas is a Time for Happy Dreams	2(	)1
Christmas is Love with all the Trimmings	3(	)1
Christmas is the Nicest Time of All	4(	)1

1   3   4

HOLLY HOBBIE – Set #HHMB
Merry Christmas

2   4

5   6   7   8

9   10   11   12

Christmas is Fun for Everyone (1977) 1 of 4	1(	)1
Christmas Brings a World of Happy Things (1977) 2 of 4	2(	)1
Christmas is Here, The Nicest Time (1977) 3 of 4	3(	)1
Christmas is for Kids of Every Age (1977) 4 of 4	4(	)1
Holidays are the Happiest Days (1978) 1 of 4 . .	5(	)1
Christmas is Magic to Your Heart (1978) 2 of 4 .	6(	)1
Dreams Come True at Christmas (1978) 3 of 4 .	7(	)1
Christmas is a Gift of Love (1978) 4 of 4	8(	)1
12 Days of Christmas – Days 1-3 (1979) 1 of 4 .	9(	)1
12 Days of Christmas – Days 4-6 (1979) 2 of 4 .	10(	)1
12 Days of Christmas – Days 7-9 (1979) 3 of 4	11(	)1
12 Days of Christmas – Days 10-12 (1979) 4 of 4	12(	)1

HOLLY HOBBIE – Set #HHAG
American Greetings Corp. – 5⅝" S.S. Heavy Base

5 1 4 3

7 6 8 9

10

Fun Is Doubled When You Share It (1978) . . . 1( )1
Happiness Starts in Sunny Hearts . . . . 2( )1
Lifes A Picnic, Enjoy It (1969) . . . . 3( )1
Light Hearted Ways Make Happy Days (1978) . 4( )1
Special Friends Give The Heart A Lift (1978) . . 5( )1
Start Each Day in a Happy Way (1972) . . . . . 6( )1
The Time To Be Happy Is Now (1967) – 5½" . . 7( )1
The World is Full of Happy Surprises (1978) . . 8( )1
Life is Filled with Sweet Surprises . . . . 9( )1
You Can't Be Poor if You Have a Friend . . . . 10( )1

HOLLY HOBBIE – Set #HHPA
On Parade Series (1976)

It's A Grand Old Day for Being Happy . . . . . . 1))1 Make Everyday a Celebration . . . . 3( )1
It's Friends That Make This Land So Grand . . . 2( )1 Three Cheers for Friendship . . . . 4( )1

HOLLY HOBBIE – Set #HHSP
Simple Pleasure Series – Coca Cola

1 2 3

4 5

Fill Your Day with Happiness	1(	)1	Make Every Day a Picnic	4(	)1
Good Friends are Like Sunshine	2(	)1	Simple Pleasurers are the Sweetest	5(	)1
Good Times are for Sharing	3(	)1	Treat The World with Tenderness	6(	)1

HOLLY HOBBIE – Set #HHCG
Heavy base – flare top – Children Christmas Scenes

1   2   3

Happy Holidays / child in front of snow man . . . 1(   )1
Joy To The World / child blowing horn . . . . . . 2(   )1
Tis The Season To Be Merry /
   child hanging stockings . . . . 3(   )1

HOLLY FARMS COLLECTOR SERIES – Set #HFC
(1975) P.A.T. Ward – Not Pepsi Brockway – 6¼"

3

Boris Badenov . . . . 1(   )6
Bullwinkle . . . . 2(   )6
Natasha . . . . 3(   )6
Rocky . . . . 4(   )6

HOOKS DRUG – Set #HOD
(1984) Donald's 50th Anniversary

2   3   5

Daisey . . . . 1(   )2
Donald . . . . 2(   )2
Goofy . . . . 3(   )2
Mickey . . . . 4(   )2
Minnie . . . . 5(   )2
Pluto . . . . 6(   )2

HOT DOG CASTLE – Set #HDC
Abilene, TX (1977)
5 11/16" S.S. Ind. Base

Abilene Future . . . . 1(   )1
Abilene Past . . . . 2(   )1
Abilene Present . . . . 3(   )1

HOWDY DOODY

KAGRAN – Set #HDK
Welches Jelly Co. – No Date

1-2-3

4-5-6

7-8-9

10-11-12

13-14-15

16-17-18

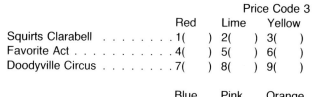

| | | Price Code 3 | |
	Red	Lime	Yellow
Squirts Clarabell	1( )	2( )	3( )
Favorite Act	4( )	5( )	6( )
Doodyville Circus	7( )	8( )	9( )

	Blue	Pink	Orange
Circus Mule	10( )	11( )	12( )
Big Shot	13( )	14( )	15( )
Tiger Trick	16( )	17( )	18( )

HOWDY DOODY – Set #HHD
(1953) Welches Jelly Co.

1-2-3-4

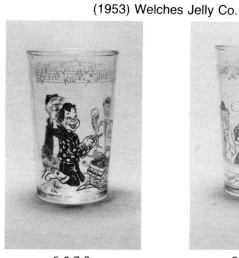

5-6-7-8

9-10-11-12

13-14-15

	Red	White	Yellow	Lime
Hits the Spot	1( )	2( )	3( )	4( )
Favorite Treat	5( )	6( )	7( )	8( )
We All Agree	9( )	10( )	11( )	12( )

	Blue	Pink	Orange
Makes You Strong . .	13( )	14( )	15( )
Like It Swell	16( )	17( )	18( )
Parade Each Day . . .	19( )	20( )	21( )

Faces on bottom of glasses are princess spring – summer – winter – fall Dilly Dally, Howdy Doody, Phinnis T. Bluster, Flub-A-Dub, and Clarabell.

16-17-18   19-20-21

INDIANA JONES MOVIES – Set #INJ
5 13/16" S.S. Creased Btm.

1-5-9-13   2-6-10-14   3-7-11-15   4-8-12-16

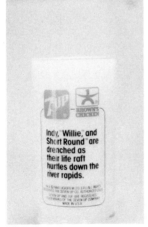

Back of Glass

	In-N-Out	Wendy's	Browns	7Up
High Priest Mola (1984) . .	1( )	5( )	9( )	13( )2
Indiana Jones with a Sword (1984)	2( )	6( )	10( )	14( )2
Indy, Willie and Short Round/Raft (1984)	3( )	7( )	11( )	15( )2
The Spiked Room (1984) . .	4( )	8( )	12( )	16( )2

JERSEY MILK PREMIUM GLASS – Set #♠JEM
Libbey Glass Co., Detroit Michigan (1930's)

Green Hornet . . . . 1(   )10+
Kato . . . . 2(   )10+

KANSAS CITY ROYALS – Set #KRC
(1977) Single Player Glass – 6¼"

| | 1 | 3 | 4 | | | 5 | 6 | |

Brett, George . . . . 1(   )3   Mayberry, John . . . . 4(   )3
Herzog, Whitey . . . . 2(   )3   McRae, Hal . . . . 5(   )3
Littell, Mark . . . . 3(   )3   Poquette, Tom . . . . 6(   )3

KANSAS CITY ROYALS – Set #KCR
5⅝" Ind. Base – United Super – MLB

George Brett/Al Cowens/Paul Splittorff . . . . 1(   )2
Amos Otis/Al Hrabosky/Larry Gura . . . . 2(   )2
Fred Patek/Dennis Leonard/Willie Wilson . . . . . . 3(   )2
Frank White/Darrell Porter/Pete LaCock . . . . 4(   )2

1   3   4   2

KEEBLER – Set #KEE
(1984) Libbey Glass Co. – 5 11/16" S.S. Ind. Base

2   4   3   1

135th Anniversary (1988) . . . . 1( )2
Ernest, Soft Batch Reminds . . . . 2( )2
Ernest, You Don't Bite Into . . . . 3( )2
Mom, Soft Batch Tastes Like . . . . 4( )2
Mom, You'd Swear These . . . . 5( )2

KELLOGG'S – Set #KEL
(1977) 4¼" Deep Ind. Base

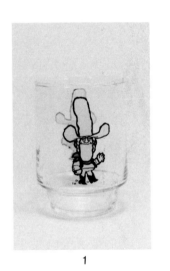

1

2

3

4

5

6

Cowboy . . . . 1( )2
Crack, Snap, Pop . . . . 2( )2
Dig Em . . . . 3( )2
Tony . . . . 4( )2
Tony, Jr. . . . . 5( )2
Toucan Sam . . . . 6( )2

KING KONG – Set #KIK
(1976) 5⅝" S.S. Ind. Base

1	2

3	4

Battles Serpent . . . . 1(   )0
Skull Island . . . . 2(   )0

Subway Train . . . . 3(   )0
Trade Towers . . . . 4(   )0

KING KONG – Set #KKF
Filmstrip – (1977) 5⅝" S.S. Ind. Base

King Kong Film Strip . . . . 1(   )2

1

KORKY KUPS CLOWN – Set #KKC
(1977) James L. Brown – 5⅝" S.S. Hvy. Base

Korky Clown – pink/green stripes . . . . 1(   )2
Korky Clown – blue/red stripes . . . . 2(   )2
Korky Clown – red/blue stripes . . . . 3(   )2

1	2	3

WALTER LANTZ – Set #LAW
No logo, white lettering

1-7

2-8

3-9

4-10

5-11

6-12

	6" Tall/Thin		5¾" Short/Thick	
Andy Panda/Miranda/Tennis	1(	)3	7(	)2
Buzz Buzzard/Space Mouse/				
Mouse chasing Buzz	2(	)3	8(	)2
Chilly Willy/Smedley/Skating	3(	)3	9(	)2
Cuddles/Oswald	4(	)3	10(	)2
Wally Walrus/Homer Pigeon	5(	)3	11(	)2
Woody/Knothead & Splinter on				
Unicycle	6(	)3	12(	)3

LEGENDS OF THE SEA – Set #LOS
(Skippers) – 5⅝"

Glass 1 Flying Dutchman as Punishment . . . . 1( )1

Glass 2 of All The Creatures Lochness Monster . 2( )1

Glass 3 in 1849 Harbor . . . . 3( )1

Glass 4 100's of Ships – Bermuda Triangle . . . 4( )1

LITTLE LULU – Set #LLL
4¾" Marge Buell (1940's)

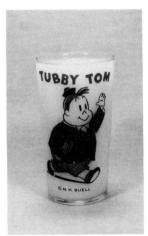

2-Front

2-Back

Little Lulu skipping rope/elephant

  "Baldy" on reverse . . . . 1( )7

Tubby Tom walking/flipper the dog on reverse . 2( )7

Alvin running/gunk on back . . . . 3( )7

Gloria front/tipper on back . . . . 4( )7

Wilbur Van Snobbe playing with yoyo/

  Nick on back . . . . 5( )7

Annie with hands on hip/Mops on back . . . . . 6( )7

LOONEY TUNES – Set #LOO
(1940's or 1950's)

Porky, blowing horn, 11 oz. blue . . . . 1(   )6
Porky, holding flower, thin 11 oz. blue . . . . . . 2(   )6
Very unusual glasses – slight flare on top.

1

2

LOONEY TUNES – Set #LTA
(Arby's) Star – (1980) – 6" Rd. Btm.

1	2	3

4	5	6

Bugs Bunny – What's Up Doc . . . . 1(   )2
Daffy duck – You're Disspicable . . . . 2(   )2
Porky Pig – That's All Folks . . . . 3(   )2

Sylvester – Sufferin Succotash . . . . 4(   )2
Tweety – I Tawt I Taw At Puddy Cat . . . . . . 5(   )2
Yosemite Sam – I'll Get That Varmint . . . . . . 6(   )2

LOONEY TUNES ADVENTURE SERIES – Set #LTS
Louisville Kentucky Arby's (1988)
5⅛" Ind. Base – Libbey Glass Co.

1-Front

1-Back

2-Front

2-Back

3-Front	3-Back	4-Front	4-Back

Bugs Bunny in "Diving for Carrots" . . . . 1( )2

Daffy Duck in "Jungle Jitters" . . . . 2( )2

Porky Pig "Lunar Lunch" . . . . 3( )2

Sylvester & Tweety in "Anchors Away" . . . . . 4( )2

LOS ANGELES DODGERS – Set #LAD
(1982) 5⅝" Rd. Btm.

Derrel Thomas . . . . 1( )1

Dusty Baker . . . . 2( )1

Fernando Valenzuela . . . . 3( )1

Pedro Guerrero . . . . 4( )1

Ron Cey . . . . 5( )1

Steve Garvey . . . . 6( )1

"LOVE IS" – Set #LOV
Los Angeles Times (1975) – 6" Rd. Btm.

1	2	3	4	5	6

Making Marriage Last 75 Years –
Tell Her She's Lovely . . . . 1( )1

Sharing Even The Hard Things –
What Ever You Make It . . . . 2( )1

Telling Him His Paint Job Is Marvelous –
Holding Ladder . . . . 3( )1

Telling Him How Much His
Golf Game Has Improved . . . . 4( )1

That First Kiss in the Morning –
Watching The Sun Sink . . . . 5( )1

Tickling His Nose with Grass –
An Autumn Walk Thru Woods . . . . 6( )1

M.A.S.H. SERIES – Set #MAS
Libbey Glass Co. – 6" Slight Flare Top

Mulcahey, Walter O'Rielly	. . . .	1( )6
Hawkeye	. . . .	2( )6
Hot Lips	. . . .	3( )6
Max Klinger, Charles Emerson Winchester	. . .	4( )6
Radar	. . . .	5( )6
Mash & 4077th – flare like coke, no logo	. . . .	6( )5

1   6   4

MCDONALDS

MCDONALDLAND ACTION – Set #MCDA
Libbey Glass Co. – Ind. Base

7-13

8-14

9-15

10-16

11-17

12-18

	1983 M's in base	1977 5 5/8"	1977 6 1/8"
Big Mac on roller skates . . .	1( )2	7( )2	13( )2
Captain Crook pulling plug out of row boat	2( )2	8( )2	14( )2
Grimace on Pogo Stick	3( )2	9( )2	15( )2
Hamburglar on a train	4( )2	10( )2	16( )2
Mayor McCheese taking pictures	5( )2	11( )2	17( )2
Ronald jumping into lake . . .	6( )2	12( )2	18( )2

MCDONALDS ADVENTURE SERIES – Set #MCDS
(1980) 6" S.S. Creased Btm.

1	2	3

Big Mac Nets Hamburglar . . . . 1(   )2
Captain Crook Sails The Bounding Main . . . . 2(   )2
Grimace Climbs A Mountain . . . . 3(   )2

4	5	6

Hamburglar Hooks Hamburger . . . . 4(   )2
Mayor McCheese and Runaway Train . . . . . . 5(   )2
Ronald McDonald Saves The Falling Star . . . . 6(   )2

MCDONALDS – Set #MCAF
Atlanta Falcons (1981)
5⅝" Ind. Base – Libbey Glass Co.

Fulton Kuykendall, Buddy Curry, Joel Williams . 1(   )2
Lynn Cain, Bobby Butler, R.C. Thielemann . . . 2(   )2
Steve Bartkowski, Alfred Jackson, Al Jenkins . . 3(   )2
William Andrewsmike Kenn, Jeff Van Note . . . 4(   )2

3	2	4	1

MCDONALDS – Set #MCCS
Camp Snoopy Collection – (1983) 6" Rd. Btm.

1	2	3	4

"Civilization If Overrated" . . . . 1( )1
"Morning People Are Hard To Love" . . . . 2( )1
"Rats, Why Is Having Fun So Much Work" . . . 3( )1
"The Struggle For Security Is No Picnic" . . . . . 4( )1
"There Is No Excuse For
  Not Being Properly Prepared" . . . . 5( )1
"Good Grief" McDonalds Camp Snoopy Glasses
  are Coming . . . . 6( )10

5

MCDONALDS – Set #MCCN
(1988) Canadian 5 9/16" Ind. Base

Birdie The Early Bird, flying . . . . 1( )2
Grimace, playing baseball . . . . 2( )2
Hamburglar, red brick road . . . . 3( )2
Ronald McDonald, in front of rainbow . . . . . . 4( )2

2   4   1   3

MCDONALD'S CHARACTER – Set #MCCA
Not Action

1   2   4   6   7   8   9

10

11

12

13

14

| | 5 1/16" | 5⅝" |
	Brockway	Indented
Mayor McCheese	1( )2	8( )1
Ronald McDonald	2( )2	9( )1
Big Mac	3( )2	10( )1
Grimace – dark blue	4( )2	11( )1
Grimace – purple	5( )2	12( )1
Captain Crook	6( )2	13( )1
Hamburglar	7( )2	14( )1
Variation – Ronald McDonald in red lettering . .	15( )3	

MCDONALDS – Set #MCDC
Walt Disney Movies – Canadian
5⅝" Coca Cola Logo

Cinderella	1( )3	Peter Pan	3( )3
Fantasia	2( )3	Seven Dwarfs	4( )3

MCDONALD DISNEYLAND – Set #MCDL
(1989) Released in Joplin, MO.
5⅝" S.S. Ind. Base – Libbey Glass Co.

1   2   3   4

Adventureland	1( )2
Critter Country	2( )2
Fantasyland	3( )2
Tomorrowland	4( )2

MCDONALDS – Set #MCGR
Garfield (1978) – Released in 1987

1   2   3   4

Are We Having Fun Yet . . . . 1(   )1
Home James . . . . 2(   )1
Just Me and the Road . . . . 3(   )1
Poetry in Motion . . . . 4(   )1

MCDONALDS GREAT MUPPET CAPER – Set #MCMC
(1981) 5⅝" S.S. Ind. Base – Libbey Glass Co.

1   2   3   4

Happiness Hotel / Bus . . . . 1(   )1   Miss Piggy / Motorcycle . . . . 3(   )1
Kermit the Frog . . . . 2(   )1   The Great Gonzo / Hot Air Balloon . . . . . . 4(   )1

MCDONALDS – Set #MCHA
Hawaii – Libbey Glass Co., 4" S.O.R.

1   2   3   4   Box and tour map with glasses

81

Bringing in the Nets	1(	)2		Sailboating	3(	)2
Canoeing	2(	)2		Surfing	4(	)2

MCDONALDS' HOUSTON – Set #MCHL
Libbey Glass Co. – Coca Cola
4¾" – Tall S.O.R. Glass

1	2	3	4

5	6	7	8

(1983) 1st of 4 – Bareback Bronc Riding,
Saddle Bronc Riding . . . . 1( )3

(1983) 2nd of 4 – Women's Barrel Racing,
Chuckwagon Races . . . . 2( )3

(1983) 3rd of 4 – Clown, Calf Scramble . . . . . 3( )3

(1983) 4th of 4 – Bull Riding, Steer Wrestling . . 4( )3

(1984) 1st of 4 – Saddle Bronc Riding,
Bareback Riding . . . . 5( )3

(1984) 2nd of 4 – Women's Barrel Racing,
Chuckwagon Races . . . . 6( )3

(1984) 3rd of 4 – Cutting Horse, Calf Scramble . 7( )3

(1984) 4th of 4 – Steer Wrestling, Bull Riding . . 8( )3

MCDONALDS MCVOTE – Set #MCMV
(1986) 5⅞" Creased Barrel

1	2	3

¼ lb Get the Votes From a Train	1(	)2
Big Mac	2(	)2
McDLT	3(	)2

MCDONALD'S – Set #MCMB
Milwaukee Brewers (1982) 5⅝"

1   2   3   4

Gorman Thomas, Cecil Cooper . . . . 1(   )2
Paul Molitor, Pete Vuckovich . . . . 2(   )2
Robin Yount, Ben Ogilvie . . . . 3(   )2
Rollie Fingers, Ted Simmons . . . . 4(   )2

MCDONALD'S – Set #MCPE
Philadelphia Eagles (1980) Libbey Glass Co.
6" – S.S. Ind. Base

1   2   3   4   5

Harold Carmichael, Randy Logan . . . . 1(   )2
John Bunting, Bill Bergey . . . . 2(   )2
Ron Jaworski, Keith Krepfle . . . . 3(   )2
Tony Franklin, Stan Walters . . . . 4(   )2
Wilbert Montgomery, Billy Campfield . . . . . . 5(   )2

MCDONALD'S – Set #MCPS
Pittsburgh Steelers Superbowl XIII
Libbey Glass Co. – 6" – S.S. Ind. Base

Jack Lambert, Sam Davis, John Banaszak . . . 1(   )2
Joe Greene, Mike Wagner, John Stallworth . . . 2(   )2
Rocky Bleier, Jack Ham, Donnie Shell . . . . . . 3(   )2
Terry Bradshaw, Mike Webster, L.C. Greenwood . 4(   )2

MCDONALD'S – Set #MCPA
Pittsburgh Steelers Superbowl XIV
5⅝" Ind. Base – Libbey Glass Co.

7   6   8   5

Jack Lambert, Jon Kolb, Mel Blount	5(	)2
Joe Greene, Matt Bahr, Sidney Thornton	6(	)2
John Stallworth, Dirt Winston, Rocky Bleier . . .	7(	)2
Terry Bradshaw, Jack Ham, Sam Davis	8(	)2

MCDONALD'S – Set #MCPB
Pittsburgh Steelers (1982) – Libbey Glass Co.
4¾" S.O.R. Glass

9   10   11   12

Mullins, Brown, Lambert, Harris, Brady, White 1 of 4	9(	)3
Greene, Nickel, Kolb, Bleier, Shell, Ham 2 of 4 .	10(	)3
Gerela, Davis, Wagner, Greenwood, Webster, Swann 3 of 4	11(	)3
Blount, Stoutner, Bradshaw, Russell, Stallworth, Butler 4 of 4	12(	)3

MCDONALD'S – Set #MCSS
Seattle Seahawks NFL – 6" (1978-1979)

1   2   3

Beeson, Eller, Beamon	1(	)3
Boyd, Gregory, Tuiasosopo	2(	)3
Raible, Zorn, McCullum	3(	)3
Smith, Largent, Sims	4(	)3

MCDONALD'S MISCELLANEOUS – Set #MCXX

1

3   11

5

15

17

3¾" Deep ind. base, McDonald's M Logo in frost
   around glass . . . . 1( )1
Baylor Bear Mascot, green/yellow . . . . 3( )3
Denim Collection, Coke, 6⅛" . . . . 5( )2
Extra, Miss Piggy Comming thru Newspaper,
   commitment date February 2, 1981. 5¾" ind. base
   "Extra! The Muppest are Coming (1981) . . . . 7( )1
Foreign Glass, Languages . . . . 9( )1
Hook'em Horns, Texas Longhorn Steer Running . 11( )3
McDonald's "No Golden Arches Logo" Set of 6 . 13( )1
World's Fair, Knoxville, TN (1982) flared . . . . . 15( )1
McTonight, hvy. base 6¼" tumbler . . . . 17( )2
Yellow Ms around 3¾" straight sided glass . . . 19( )1

MARK TWAIN COUNTRY SERIES – Set #MTC
Burger King

Huck Finn . . . . 1( )2
Tom Sawyer . . . . 2( )2
Mark Twain . . . . 3( )2
Octagonal Study . . . . 4( )2

MARRIOTT'S – Set #MAR
Short Glass, No Moon (1973) – Warner Bro. 4¾"

Bug's Bunny . . . . 1( )2
Road Runner . . . . 2( )2
Sylvester . . . . 3( )2
Wilie E Coyote . . . . 4( )2

MARRIOTT'S – Set #MRR
Short Glass with Moon (1975) 4¾"

Bugs Bunny – orange moon, blk. letters . . . . . 1( )2
Road Runner – golden yellow, blk. letters . . . . 2( )2
Road Runner – golden yellow, red letters . . . . 3( )2
Sylvester – golden yellow, blk. letters . . . . . . 4( )2
Sylvester – golden yellow, red letters . . . . . . 5( )2
Wilie E Coyote – golden yellow, blk. letters . . . 6( )2
Wilie E Coyote – golden yellow, red letters . . . 7( )2

MARRIOTT'S GREAT AMERICA – Set #MGA
(1982) Rd. Btm. 4 11/16" – S.S. Hvy. Base

Bugs Bunny . . . . 1( )1
Honey Bunny . . . . 2( )1
Tweety . . . . 3( )1
Honey Bear . . . . 4( )1
Sylvester . . . . 5( )1

MARVEL COMICS – Set #MAV
(1977) Distributed by 7-11
5⅝" S.S. Ind. Base

1

2

3

4

5

6

Amazing Spiderman	1(	)3
Captain America and Falcon	2(	)2
Fantastic Four	3(	)2
Howard the Duck	4(	)2
Incredible Hulk	5(	)2
Mighty Thor	6(	)2

MARVEL COMICS – Set #MAC
(1978) Federal Glass – 16 oz.
No Shield or Bottling Co. Logo

1

2

4

5

Captain America	1(	)6	Spiderman	4(	)6
Hulk	2(	)6	Thor	5(	)6
Spiderwoman	3(	)6			

MASTERS OF THE UNIVERSE – Set #MTU
Mattel, Inc. – Libbewy Glass Co.
5⅝" S.S. Ind. Base

1

2

3

4

5

6

7

8

	1983 16 oz.	1986 7 oz.			
He-Man	1( )3	5( )2	Orko		7( )2
Man-At-Arms	2( )3	6( )2	Skeletor & Panthor	3( )3	8( )2
			Teela	4( )3	

MISSION SERIES – Set #MMS
5 9/16" S.S. Ind. Base – Coca Cola

4   1   5

6   2   3

MISTER MAGOO – Set #MRM
UPA Pictures Inc.

2   1   3   5

6   7

(1964) UPA, lt. blue band – In Old Car Saying "Road Hog"
and on a Cow Backwards Saying, "Giddiyap"
orange 4¼" . . . . 6( )5

(1961) UPS, yellow band btm. – Parachute,
What A Crazy Ride in Old Car Saying Road Hog
in lt. blue 4 9/16" . . . . 1( )5
(1961) UPA, red band, Magoo in grey, Tipping Hat to a
Fire Hydrant, Holding Balloons,
Shotgun Duck Falling 4 9/16" . . . . 2( )5
(1962) UPA, lt. blue band – Shows Magoo Walking in a
Manhole While Call a Taxi, other side on
Horse Backwards . . . . 3( )5
(1962) UPA, lt. blue band btm. – Giddiyap – 5 9/16"
rd. btm. tapered in top, hvy. rim yellow top
and pink top . . . . 4( )5
(1963) UPS, lt. band – Shows Magoo Going Down a Ski
Slope Backwards and
Where's The Beach in the Arctic . . . . 5( )5
(1964) UPA, pink band btm. – Road Hog/Giddiyap
hvy. tapered glass, pink band blue top . . . . . 7( )5

MOBIL OIL – Set #MOB
NFL Helments 5 9/16" – Ind. Base
Libbey Glass Co. (1988)

27   13   6   19   14

New York Jets	. . . .	17(	)1	Pittsburgh Steelers	. . . .	23(	)1
New York Giants	. . . .	18(	)1	San Francisco 49'ers	. . . .	24(	)1
New Orleans Saints	. . . .	19(	)1	San Diego Chargers	. . . .	25(	)1
New England Patriots	. . . .	20(	)1	Seattle Seahawks	. . . .	26(	)1
Phoenix Cardinals	. . . .	21(	)1	Tampa Bay Buccaneers	. . . .	27(	)1
Phildelphia Eagles	. . . .	22(	)1	Washington Redskins	. . . .	28(	)1

MONTREAL EXPOS – Set #MNT
MLB (1984) 5⅝"

4   1   2   3

7   6   5

Andre Dawson #10	. . . .	1(	)2	Peter Rose #14	. . . .	5(	)2
Bill Gullickson #34	. . . .	2(	)2	Steve Rogers #45	. . . .	6(	)2
Charlie Lea #53	. . . .	3(	)2	Tim Raines #30	. . . .	7(	)2
Gary Carter #8	. . . .	4(	)2				

MORRIS THE CAT – Set #MOR
By 9 Lives

2   1

Morris saying "Morris On Glass Is Like
Sterling on Silver" . . . . 1( )2
Morris saying "There's Something Irresistible
About This Glass" . . . . 2( )2

MOTHER'S PIZZA – Set #MOP
Coca Cola 5⅞" Flare – Canadian

1 of 6 Girl and Motorcycle . . . . 1( )2
2 of 6 Airplae and Train . . . . 2( )2
3 of 6 Girl Dancing – Gay 90's . . . . 3( )2
4 of 6 Old Car . . . . 4( )2
5 of 6 Baseball Player . . . . 5( )2
6 of 6 Trump Player . . . . 6( )2

MOVIE STARS – Set #MSA
Arby's (1979) – Libbey Glass Co.
5⅝" S.S. Ind. Base

1

2

3

4

5

6

Charlie Chaplin 1 of 6 . . . . 1(   )2
Abbott and Costello 2 of 6 . . . . 2(   )2
Laurel and Hardy 3 of 6 . . . . 3(   )2
Mae West 4 of 6 . . . . 4(   )2
Lil Rascals 5 of 6 . . . . 5(   )2
W. C. Fields 6 of 6 . . . . 6(   )2

MOVIE STARS – Set #MOS
No Logo

Clark Gable . . . . 1(   )2   Marilyn Monroe . . . . 4(   )2
Humphrey Bogart . . . . 2(   )2   Theda Bara . . . . 5(   )2
Jean Harlow . . . . 3(   )2   W.C. Fields . . . . 6(   )2

MOVIE STARS OF THE ROARING 20'S – Set #MSS
3⅜" S.O.R. Glass – No Logo

1

2

3

4

Buster Keaton/Lionel Barrymore/Tom Mix . . . . 1( )1	Douglas Fairbanks/Rudolph Valentino/
Charlie Chaplin/John Barrymore/Clara Bow . . . 2( )1	Laurel & Harvey . . . . 3( )1
	Mary Pickford/Raymond Novarro/Harold Lloyd . 4( )1

MOVIE STARS – Set #MSC
Soda Glass – Coke

Jack Albertson . . . . 1( )2	Mary Tyler Moore . . . . 4( )2
Monty Hall . . . . 2( )2	Jan Murry . . . . 5( )2
Teddy Kollack . . . . 3( )2	Don Rickles . . . . 6( )2

NATIONAL PUBLICATIONS, INC. – Set #NPS
No Year (Words Zok, Wack, Craack)
5 1/16" S.S. Tapered Body

1

2

Batman . . . . 1( )3
Robin The Boy Wonder . . . . 2( )3

NEBRASKA CORNHUSKERS – Set #NBC
(1976) 5⅞" Rd. Btm. Sam's

Hawaii Rainbows . . . . 1( )2	Miami University Hurricanes . . . . 7( )2
Indiana Hoosiers . . . . 2( )2	Missouri Tigers . . . . 9( )2
Iowa State University Cyclones . . . . 3( )2	Oklahoma State University Cowboys . . . . . . 10( )2
Kansas Jayhawks . . . . 4( )2	Oklahoma University Sooners . . . . 11( )2
Kansas State Wildcats . . . . 5( )2	TCU Frog's . . . . 12( )2
Louisiana State University Tigers . . . . 6( )2	Nebraska (1975) Record/Go Big Red . . . . . . 13( )2

NEW YORK ISLANDERS – Set #NYI
Ice Hockey – 7-11 (1976)

Trottier . . . . 1( )1	Nystrom . . . . 2( )1

NOID'S – Set #NOD
Dominos' Pizza (1988) Will Vinton Prod. – 5" S.S.
Indented Btm. – Libbey Glass Co.

1

2

3

4

Noid on Skis	1(	)2
Noid Playing Golf	2(	)2
Noid Playing Tennis	3(	)2
Noid Sitting in Beach Chair	4(	)2
Noid Christmas – S.O.R. Glass 4⅛"	5(	)2

5

NURSERY RHYMES (1930's – 1940's – 1950's)

NURSERY RHYMES – Set #NRY
4" glass with internal ribs in glass,
like the old Garrett Snuff glasses
⅝" rim at top – solid color

A Frog, He Would – red	1(	)2
Doodle Doodle Doo – red	2(	)2
Goosey Goosey Garder – white	3(	)2
Gulliver – red	4(	)2
Little Boy Blue – blue	5(	)2
Little Jack Horner – red	6(	)2
Mary Had A Little Lamb – white	7(	)2
Old King Cole – white	8(	)2
Old Mother Goose – blue	9(	)2
Old Mother Hubbard – white	10(	)2
Pussy Cat Pussy Cat – blue	11(	)2
Simple Sam – red	12(	)2
Simple Simon – red	13(	)2
The Queen of Hearts – yellow	14(	)2
There Was An Old Woman – green	15(	)2
These Little Pigs – green	16(	)2
Tom Tom The Pipers Son	17(	)2

2   9   13

NURSERY RHYMES – Set #NRY
4⅜" – Thin like an early Libbey Glass

Old King Cole – light green . . . . 20( )2   Rub-a-Dub – all red . . . . 21( )2

NURSERY RHYMES – Set #NRY
4⅝" Libbey Glass – 2½" mouth opening
solid color – vertical name

Jack and Jill – pinkish	26(	)2
Jack Is Nimble – green	27(	)2
Little Bo-Peep – red	28(	)2
Little Boy Blue – light blue	29(	)2
Little Miss Muppet – red	30(	)2
Mary Had A Little Lamb – light blue	31(	)2
Mistress Mary – white	32(	)2
Old Mother Hubbard – orange	33(	)2

28   31   27   29

NURSERY RHYMES – Set #NRY
4⅝" Federal Glass – 2½" M.O. – solid color

38   41   39

Little Bo-Peep – red . . . . 37(   )2
Little Jack Horner – mauve type pink color . . . 38(   )2
Little Miss Muffet – mauve type pink color . . . . 39(   )2
Little Boy Blue – blue . . . . 40(   )2
Mistress Mary – yellow . . . . 41(   )2
Mary Had A Little Lamb – light blue . . . . 42(   )2
Jack Is Nimble – green . . . . 43(   )2

NURSERY RHYMES – Set #NRY
4 13/16" medium weight glass – destintive rim glass
white outline character

The Queen of Hearts . . . . 46(   )2   Tom, Tom, The Piper's Son . . . . 47(   )2

NURSERY RHYMES – Set #NRY
4 7/16" medium thickness and base
like a small Brockway Glass 2 7/16" M.O.

53   55

Hickety Pickety, single color yellow . . . . 52(   )2
Jack Sprat, white with red btm. border . . . . . . 53(   )2
Little Boy Blue, single color blue . . . . 54(   )2
Peter Piper, white with blue flowers at bottom . . 55(   )2

NURSERY RHYMES – Set #NRY
4⅞" Glass with heavy base – Multi-color
Action Series, 2⅜" M.O.

64   63   61   62   60

Humpty Dumpty . . . . 60(   )2
Jack and Jill . . . . 61(   )2
Little Boy Blue . . . . 62(   )2
Old King Cole . . . . 63(   )2
Old Woman in Shoe . . . . 64(   )2

NURSERY RHYMES – Set #NRY
4 9/16" Hazel Atlas Glass – large rounded lip
2¼" M.O.

54   52   70

Jack and Jill, all in red . . . . 70(   )2

NURSERY RHYMES – Set #NRY
4 11/16" Heavy type glass with a letter and number
in bottom – solid color – 2 7/16" M.O.

83   81   84   79

Humpty Dumpty, yellow . . . . 78(   )2
Jack and Jill, dark green . . . . 79(   )2
Little Bo-Peep, blue . . . . 80(   )2
Little Boy Blue, blue . . . . 81(   )2
Little Jack Horner, red . . . . 82(   )2
Old King Cole, red . . . . 83(   )2
Old Woman in Shoe, yellow . . . . 84(   )2

NURSERY RHYMES – Set #NRY
5" Glass with Heavy Base – Multi-color
Action Series 2 11/16" M.O.

88   87   89

Jack Be Nimble . . . . 87(   )2
Mistress Mary . . . . 88(   )2
Ring Around The Rosy . . . . 89(   )2

NURSERY RHYMES – Set #NRY
5" thick hvy. base glass – 2½" M.O.

20   21   94   93

Little Miss Muffet – white and tanish color . . . . 93( )2
Wee Willie Winkie, sky blue one color . . . . . . 94( )2

NURSERY RHYMES – Set #NRY
5" thick heavy base glass – 2¾" M.O.

Little Bo-Peep, pea green . . . . 99( )2
Little Boy Blue, blue . . . . 100( )2

Wee Willie Winkle, teal blue . . . . 101( )2

NURSERY RHYMES – Set #NRA
Alphabet Glasses

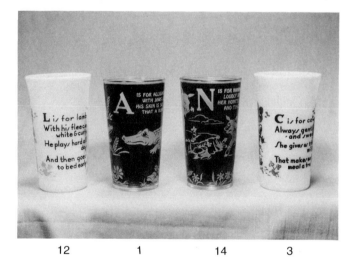

12   1   14   3

A – is for Alligator . . . . 1( )1
B – is for Bunny . . . . 2( )1
C – is for Cow . . . . 3( )1
D – is for Donkey . . . . 4( )1
E – is for Elephant . . . . 5( )1
I – is for Ibex . . . . 9( )1
J – is for Jaguar . . . . 10( )1
L – is for Lamb . . . . 12( )1
N – is for Nanny-Goat . . . . 14( )1
O – is for Opossum . . . . 15( )1
R – is for Raccoon . . . . 18( )1
X – is for Xema . . . . 23( )1

N.Y. TIMES – Set #NYT
4⅛" hvy base, S.O.R. glass – Wendy's

3   2   1

Columbia Returns . . . . 1( )1
Men Land on the Moon . . . . 2( )1
Nation and Millions in City . . . . 3( )1
U.S. Defeats Soviet Squad . . . . 4( )1

OKLAHOMA INDIANS – Set #OKI
By Acee Blue Eagle – Knox Gas Promotion
Late 1950's

1 – 8

9 – 16

	5¼" Clear	6 9/16" Frosted
Bacon Rind, Osage	1( )3	9( )2
Dull Knife, Cheyenne	2( )3	10( )2
Geronimo, Apache	3( )3	11( )2
Hen-Toh, Wyandot	4( )3	12( )2

Pitcher, "Oklahoma,		
Home of the Red Man	5( )3	13( )2
Quanah Parker, Comanche . . .	6( )3	14( )2
Ruling His Sun, Pawnee	7( )3	15( )2
Sequoyah, Cherokee	8( )3	16( )2

OKLAHOMA CITY WORLD CHAMPION
RODEO SERIES – Set #OCR
(1979) National Finals

Bareback Riding	1( )1	Saddle Bronc Riding	4( )1
Bull Riding	2( )1	Steer Wrestling	5( )1
Calf Roping	3( )1	Team Roping	6( )1

OLYMPIC GAMES – Set #OLG
Double Crease 5¾"

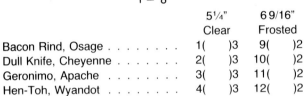

1

2

3

4

Amsterdam (1928)	1( )1	Mexico (1968)	3( )1
Germany Berlin (1936)	2( )1	Munchen (1972)	4( )1

PPMR – 1   ACR – 5

ALC

3   2   1

ARB

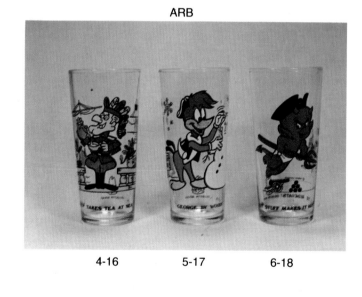

1-11-12   2-13   3-14-15

ARB

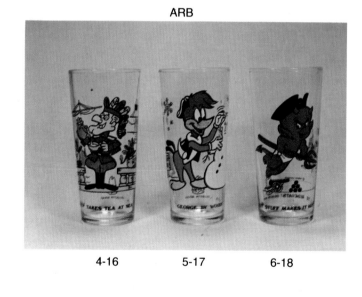

4-16   5-17   6-18

ARB

7-19   8-20   9-21   10-22

BLO

1   2   3

BLO

4   5   6

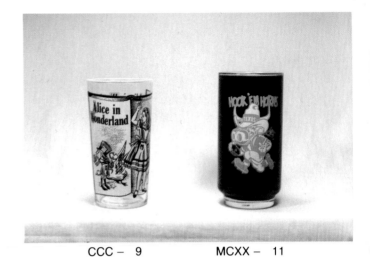

CCC – 9   MCXX – 11

CMS

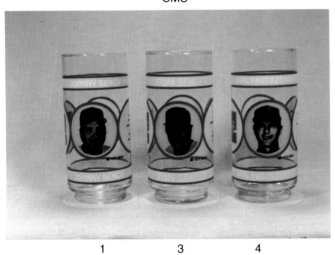

1   3   4

DRW

1   2   3   4

DTR

1   2   3   4

HAR

1   2   3   4

COLOR ILLUSTRATIONS
Details in Black & White Section

HDA

HDA

3 2

6 7 5

LLL – 1 MGX – 25

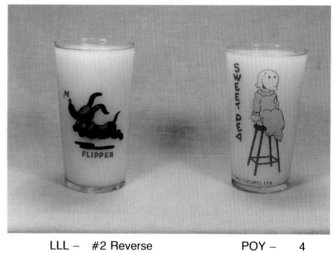

LLL – #2 Reverse POY – 4

MCXX

MNT

5 3

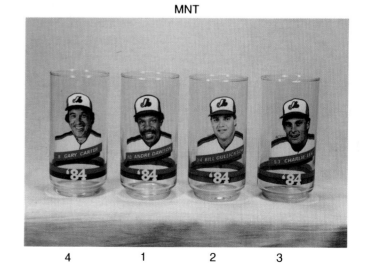

4 1 2 3

C

COLOR ILLUSTRATIONS
Details in Black & White Section

PAX – 5   LAW – 4

PFC

Not Numbered   4

PHBM

1-9   2-10   3-11   4-12

PJBO

1   2   3   4

POP

1   2   3   4

PRES

1   2   3

COLOR ILLUSTRATIONS
Details in Black & White Section

PRES

4   5   6

PRES

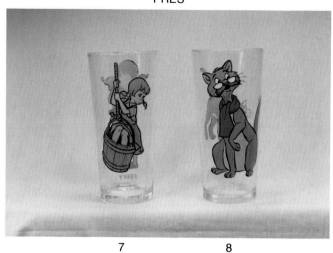

7   8

PSCS

1   2   3   4

PSCS

5   6   7   8

PSCS

9   10

PSHC

9   10   11

COLOR ILLUSTRATIONS
Details in Black & White Section

PSHC

12   13   14

PSHD

1-4

PSS

1   2   3   4

PSX – 24   HGR – 1

PWBF – 26   PWBB – 28

PWLG

1   2-7   3

F

COLOR ILLUSTRATIONS
Details in Black & White Section

PWLG

4   5   11-6-9

STM

1   2   3

1978

5-8

UNI

3   5   1

UNI

8   7   6   9

WDDD

3   1   2

COLOR ILLUSTRATIONS
Details in Black & White Section

WDFB

| 1-7 | 2-8 | 3-9 |

WDFB

| 4-10 | 5-11 | 6-12 |

WDK

PHCS – 15

| 1 | 2 | 3 | 4 |

TRR – 1

| WDSN – 57 | SUN – 2 |

WDSC

| 21 | 23 | 43 |

H

OLYMPICS SAM THE EAGLE – Set #OLS
(1980) Coca Cola set of twelve or more – 6¾" – .4L

5	7	8	9

Boxing	1( )1		Swimming	6( )1
Diving	2( )1		Talking	7( )1
Gymnastics	3( )1		Torch	8( )1
Hurdles	4( )1		Soccer	9( )1
Kayak Racing	5( )1			

OREGON KAMIKAZE BASKETBALL – Set #OKB
Kugn 590 – R.C. Cola – 5⅝"

Ernie Kent	1( )1		Mike Drummand	4( )1
Greg Ballard	2( )1		Ron Le	5( )1
Mark Barwig	3( )1		Stu Jackson	6( )1

PACMAN – Set #PAC
(1980) AAFES

1	3	4

Bashful, blue	1( )1
Pokey, yellow	2( )1
Shadow, red	3( )1
Speedy, pink	4( )1

PACMAN MISCELLANEOUS – Set #PAX

| 4 | 5 | 6 |

Pacman, flare top (1980) Bally 5¼" high . . . . . 1( )1
Pacman, flare top Bally 5½" . . . . 2( )1
Pacman, flare top Bally 3½" . . . . 3( )1
Pacman, flare top (1982) Bally 6" High . . . . . 4( )1

Pacman, no flare, Arby's Collector's
Series Bally (1980) 4⅝" hvy. base . . . . 5( )1
Pacman, no flare, Bally 5" high no date . . . . . 6( )1

PARAMOUNT PICTURES INC. – Set #PAR
Copyright (1939) – Different sizes and shapes

	4¾"	5⅛"
Bombo, character is brown	1( )6	13( )7
Gulliver, character is orange . . .	2( )6	14( )7
Gulliver, character is red	3( )6	15( )7
Sneak, character is brown	4( )6	16( )7
Snitch in red	5( )6	17( )7
Snoop, character is brown	6( )6	18( )7
Twinkletoes in red	7( )6	19( )7
Prince David	8( )6	20( )7
Princess Gloria	9( )6	21( )7
King Little	10( )6	22( )7
Gabby	11( )6	23( )7
. . . .	12( )6	24( )7

| 7-19 | 6-18 | 4 1/16" Misc. | 2-14 | 1-13 |

PEANUT'S – Set #PSC
Snoopy Election (1958)
Released in 1988 – 5⅞" Rd. Btm.

Back The Beagle . . . . 1( )1
Put Snoopy In The White House . . . . 2( )1
The People's Choice . . . . 3( )1
Vote for the American Beagle . . . . 4( )1

| 2 | 1 | 3 | 4 |

PEANUT'S – Set #PSS
Snoopy Sport – 6⅛" S.S. Crease Btm.

1	2	3	4

Snoopy, Baseball . . . . 1(   )2   Snoopy, Golf . . . . 3(   )2

Snoopy, Football . . . . 2(   )2   Snoopy, Tennis . . . . 4(   )2

PEANUTS – Set #PSK
Snoopy (1988) Krafts' Jelly

1	2	**3**	**4**

Charlie Brown flying kite . . . . 1(   )1   Snoopy on surfboard . . . . 3(   )1

Lucy on swing . . . . 2(   )1   Snoopy, Woodstock floating in pool . . . . 4(   )1

PEANUTS CHARACTERS – Set #PSX
Miscellaneous – UFS

3	6	15	21

99

BBQ for Peanuts Gang	1( )1
Charlie Brown and Lucy, never under estimate pretty face	3( )1
Charlie Brown flying a kite – 5 3/16" curved ind. base	6( )1
Lucy jumping rope, friends 5¼"	9( )1
Lucy's lemonade stand 5¼" ind. base	10( )1
Peanut's gang enjoying sunshine, clouds and grass	12( )1
Snoopy and big apple	15( )1
Snoopy eating submarine sandwich and spaghetti 16 oz.	18( )1
Snoopy – hamburger, fries, hotdog	21( )1
Snoopy's kitchen, Charlie Brown and Lucy coming to eat	24( )1
Snoopy's juice pitcher, kitchen	26( )1

24   26

PEPSI COLA COLLECTORS SERIES

PEPSI – Set #PCAN
75th Anniversary (with shaker)

	3 9/16" S.O.R. 12 oz.	5 9/16" 16 oz.
(1898)	1( )6	7( )6
(1905)	2( )6	8( )6
(1906)	3( )6	9( )6
(1950)	4( )6	10( )6
(1962)	5( )6	11( )6
(1973)	6( )6	12( )6

1-12

BASEBALL PAST GREATS – Set #PBPG
United Oil 5 1/16" (1988) Rd. Btm.

Babe Ruth (1936)	1( )3
Lou Gerhig	2( )3
Roberto Clemente (1973)	3( )3
Ty Cobb	4( )3

3   4   2

CALLAHANS – Set #PCAL
Pepsi 5⅝" Short ind. – Elfried Monaco Copyright

2   1

The Blues Burgers . . . . 1( )5
The Fried Pipers . . . . 2( )5

CATERPILLAR TRACTOR – Set #PCAT
Rd. Btm. 6"

1   2

Tractor Glass #1.D 8 L (1908) . . . . 1( )2
Tractor Glass #2.16 G (1931) . . . . 2( )2
Tractor Glass – Variation, Caterpillar, Mis-spelled . 3( )2

Glasses were released on the East Coast. Each glass has a picture of a present day tractor and a tractor of the past.

CHRISTMAS POEM SERIES – Set #PCPM
6"

1   2   3   4

	1983 Rd. Btm.	1982 Crease
Mouse in Bed, Dec. 24th	1( )2	5( )2
Reindeers Over Roof Tops	2( )2	6( )2
Santa on Sleigh Waving	3( )2	7( )2
Stockings on Fireplace	4( )2	8( )2

CHRISTMAS SONG SERIES – Set #PCSO
Collection Pepsi – rd. btm. 6"

| | 1-5 | 2-6 | 3-7 | 4-8 |

	1983	1984				
Jingle Bells	1( )2	5( )2	Toyland	3( )2	7( )2
O Christmas Tree	2( )2	6( )2	We Wish You A Merry Christmas .	4( )2	8( )2

THE 12 DAYS OF CHRISTMAS – Set #PCDA
Pepsi

| 1 | 2 | 3 | 4 |

| 5 | 6 | 7 | 8 |

9

10

11

12

13

	16 oz. Thick	Rd. Bottom
1st Day	1( )1	13( )1
2nd Day	2( )1	14( )1
3rd Day	3( )1	15( )1
4th Day	4( )1	16( )1
5th Day	5( )1	17( )1
6th Day	6( )1	18( )1
7th Day	7( )1	19( )1
8th Day	8( )1	20( )1
9th Day	9( )1	21( )1
10th Day . . . . 10( )1	22( )1	
11th Day	11( )1	23( )1
12th Day	12( )1	24( )1

PEPSI – Set #PCCC
Circa – Color Cap

2   3   4

CLEMSON COLLEGE TIGERS – Set #PCCG
Rd. Btm.

Go Tigers (Helmet Over Clemson)	1(	)3
Go Tigers (Record Through 1974)	2(	)3

(1906)	1(	)4
(1950)	2(	)4
(1962)	3(	)4
(1973)	4(	)4

DETROIT RED WINGS – Set #PDRW
Total Oil S.S. Ind. Base 12 oz.

Bob Probert	1(	)3
Brent Ashton	2(	)3
Harold Snepsts	3(	)3
Steve Yzerman	4(	)3

WALT DISNEY – Set #PHBM
Happy Birthday Mickey Series – Brockway Glass Co.
16 oz. thick 6 5/16"

2-10   1-9   3-11   4-12

5-13   6-14   7-15   8-16

Daisy and Donald	1(	)7	9(	)3			
Donald	2(	)5	10(	)2			
Goofy	3(	)5	11(	)2			
Horace and Clarabelle	4(	)7	12(	)3			

Mickey	5(	)5	13(	)2
Minnie	6(	)5	14(	)2
Pluto	7(	)5	15(	)2
Uncle Scrooge	8(	)5	16(	)2

WALT DISNEY – Set #PJBO
(1977) Jungle Book – Brockway Glass Co.
16 oz., thick

1

2

3

4

5

6

7

8

Bagheera (Blue Leopard)	. . . .	1(	)5
Baloo (Bear/Juggling)	. . . .	2(	)5
Colonel Hathi (Elephant)	. . . .	3(	)5
KAA (Snake)	. . . .	4(	)6
King Louie (Gorilla)	. . . .	5(	)6

Mowgli (Boy)	. . . .	6(	)5
Rama (Wolf)	. . . .	7(	)5
Shere Kahn (Tiger)	. . . .	8(	)5
Bagheera, clear face, variation	. . . .	9(	)5

WALT DISNEY – Set #PRES
(1977) The Rescuers – Brockway Glass Co.
16 oz., thick – 6¼"

1

2

3

4

5

6

7

8

Bernard	. . . .	1(	)4
Bianca	. . . .	2(	)4
Brutus and Nero	. . . .	3(	)4
Evinrude	. . . .	4(	)4

Madame Medusa	. . . .	5(	)4
Orville	. . . .	6(	)4
Penny	. . . .	7(	)4
Rufus	. . . .	8(	)5

WALT DISNEY – Set #PSRB
(1979) Single Character – Rd. Btm. 6"

1

2

3

4

5

6

Daisy	1(	)2
Donald	2(	)2
Goofy	3(	)2
Mickey	4(	)2
Minnie	5(	)2
Pluto	6(	)3

WALT DISNEY – Set #PTAP
(Texas Series) Action Scenes – Rd. Btm. 6"

1

2

3

4

5

6

Daisy/Pie/3 Boys/Baseball & Bat	1(	)2
Donald/Net/Scrooge/Money/3 Boys	2(	)2
Goofy/Shovel/Digging Hole	3(	)5
Mickey/Grocery Basket/Goofy/BBQ/Pluto .	4(	)2
Minnie/Laundry/Mickey as Cowboy	5(	)2
Pluto/Morty Sailing	6(	)5

WALT DISNEY – Set #PDWW
Wonderful World – Rd. Btm. 6"

1

2

3

4

5

6

101 Dalmations	1(	)2
Alice In Wonderland	2(	)2
Bambi	3(	)2
Lady & The Tramp	4(	)2
Pinocchio	5(	)2
Snow White	6(	)2

ET – Set #PETM
By MCA Home Video And Amblin Ent.
Universal Studio (1982) – 5 9/16"

ET' Finger Glowing	1(	)2	ET – Rides with Elliott	4(	)2
ET – Dressed Up	2(	)2	Elliott Hug's ET	5(	)2
Gerttie Kisses ET	3(	)2	ET – Say's Good Buy	6(	)2

FRIENDS ARE US – Set #PFAU
(Visual Creations) 16 oz. Thick – 6 5/16"
Brockway Glass Co.

1-7

2-8

3-9

4-10

5-11

6-12

	Pepsi Logo			
	With		Without	
Camel (You're Too Nice To Forget)	1(	)5	7(	)2
Giraffe (You Give Me A Lift) . . .	2(	)5	8(	)2
Monkey (Friends Like You Are Very Few)	3(	)5	9(	)2
Do Do Bird (I'm Glad We're Friends)	4(	)5	10(	)2
Owl (I Only Have Eyes For You) .	5(	)5	11(	)2
Tiger (Knowing You Makes Me Feel Good All Over)	6)	)5	12(	)2

PEPSI – Set #PGOA
Grand Opening's and Anniversary Glasses

1

5

9

19

11

15

25

29

31-Front

31-Back

HANNA BARBERA – Set #PHBR
Brockway Glass Co. (1977) – 16 oz.
Thick 6 5/16"

1

2

3

4

5

6

Dynomutt	1(	)3
Josie & The Pussycats	2(	)3
Mumbly	3(	)4
Scooby Doo	4(	)4
The Flintstones	5(	)3
Yogi Bear & Huck	6(	)3

HARVEY CARTOON SERIES – Set #PHCC
Brockway Glass Co. 6¼"

1-8

2-9

3-4-10

5

6

7-11

	16 oz.		12 oz.	
Thick	WL		5⅛"	
Big Baby Huey	1(	)2	8(	)2
Casper . . . . blue l. 2( )2			9(	)1
Hot Stuff . . . . black 3( )2	4(	)2	10(	)2
Richie Rich	5(	)2		
Sad Sack	6(	)4		
Wendy	7(	)2	11(	)2
Variation				
Big Baby Huey, no white, no name . . . . . . 12(	)3			

HARVEY CARTOON – Set #PHCS
6⅛" S.S. Ind. Base

13   15   16

Big Baby Huey, no logo, straight sides . . . . . 13( )4
Casper, no logo, straight sides . . . . 14( )4
Hot Stuff, no logo, straight sides . . . . 15( )4
Richie Rich, no logo straight sides . . . . 16( )4

HARVEY CARTOON SERIES – Set #PHCA
Action 12 oz. Thick 5 1/16" – Brockway Glass Co.

1   2   3   4

Big Baby Huey (Barbells) . . . . 1( )3   Hot Stuff (Going Through Fence) . . . . 3( )3
Casper (Haunted House) . . . . 2( )3   Wendy (Stirring Pot) . . . . 4( )3

WALTER LANTZ – Set #PWLG
Brockway Glass Co.

1   2-7   3   4

5

8

10

11-6-9

	6 5/16" 16 oz. Thick WL	5⅛" 12 oz.
Andy Panda	1( )8	
Chilly Willy	2( )4	7( )2
Chilly Willy (Action) Painting Snowman		8( )3

	6 5/16" BL	16 oz. WL	5⅛" 12 oz.
Cuddles		3( )3	
Space Mouse		4( )10+	
Wally Walrus		5( )3	
Woody Woodpecker BL 11( )3	6( )3		9( )2
Woody Woodpecker (Action) Chasing Butterfly			10( )3

LEONARDO TTV – Set #PLTT
Pepsi – Brockway Glass Co.

5

4-8-11

3-15

2-7-10

1-6-9

12

	6 5/16"	16 oz. Thick		5⅛" 12 oz.
		BL	WL	
Go Go Gopher		5( )3		
Simon Bar Sinister	1( )3	6( )3		9( )3
Sweet Polly	2( )4	7( )4		10( )3
Underdog (large logo) blue .	3( )4			
Underdog (small logo)	4( )2	8( )2		11( )2
Underdog Action (phone booth) . .		12( )3		
VARIATIONS				
Simon Bar Sinister – No Leonardo TTV				13( )3
Sweet Polly – No Leonardo TTV				14( )3
Under Dog – No logo – 16 oz. – blue name				15( )3

M.G.M. – Set #PMGM
(1975) Action 12 oz. Thick – 5⅛"

1

2

Jerry (Catching Tom's tail in mousetrap) . . . . . 1(   )3
Tom (Chasing Jerry into mousehole) . . . . . . 2(   )3

M.G.M. – Set #PMGC
16 oz. thick – Brockway Glass 6 5/16"

1-7

2-8

3-9

4-10

5-11-12

6-13

	BL		WL	
Barney	1(	)2	7(	)1
Droopy	2(	)2	8(	)1
Jerry	3(	)2	9(	)2
Spike	4(	)2	10(	)2
Tom	5(	)2	11(	)2
Tom, gray/green body			12(	)4
Tuffy	6(	)2	13(	)2

OHIO BICENTENNIAL – Set #POBI
5⅛" Thick

Fort Amanda/Fort Findlay . . . . 1(   )2
Tecumseh/Johnny Appleseed . . . . 2(   )2
Train/Miami/Erie Canal . . . . 3(   )2

1   2   3

P.A.T. WARD PRODUCTIONS – Set #PPAT
Brockway Glass Co.

1-11

18   19

2-3-4-12-20-26-29

13-5-14-21-30

6-15-22-32

7-34

8-9-16-23

	31		27		10-17-24-36

	6 5/16" 16 oz. Thick		5 1/8" 12 oz.	
	Blk	WL	Blk	
Boris & Natasha	1( )2	11( )2		Rocky (sm. logo)
Boris Badenov			18( )3	Br L ...... 8( )4 9( )2 16( )2 23( )1
Natasha			19( )3	Snidley Wiplash
Bullwinkle (lg. logo) Br L .	2( )3 3( )2			green L .... 10( )3 17( )3 24( )2
Bullwinkle (sm. logo) ...	4( )2	12( )2	20( )2	VARIATIONS
Dudley-Do-Right (lg. logo)		13( )2		Bullwinkle – No P.A.T. Ward – white .... 26( )3
Dudley-Do-Right (sm. logo) ...	5( )2	14))2	21( )2	Bullwinkle – Small Horn, no logo, brown ..... 27( )5
Mr. Peabody ..	6( )2	15( )2	22( )2	Bullwinkle – No P.A.T. Ward w/logo, black .... 29( )3
Rocky (lg. logo) gray L .....7( )4				Dudley-Do-Right, No logo, red letters .... 30( )5
				Dudley-Do-Right, Hat Tipper, lg. logo, white .... 31( )4
				Mr. Peabody, No P.A.T. Ward with logo, white .. 32( )3
				Rocky, no logo, like greay but brown .... 34( )6
				Snidley Whiplish – No P.A.T. Ward .... 36( )4

P.A.T. WARD PRODUCTIONS – Set #PPAA
Action 12 oz. Thick – 5⅛

1   2   3

Bullwinkle (Balloons) .... 1( )3
Dudley-Do-Right (Canoe) .... 2( )3
Rocky (Circus Tent) .... 3( )3

PANCHOS MEXICAN RESTAURANT – Set #PPMR
Texas

	Pepsi Logo Thick	No Pepsi logo Rd. Bottom Yellow Hat	Red Hat
Pancho (black outfit) . . .	1( )4	2( )2	3( )3

2   1   3

POPEYE'S FAMOUS FRIED CHICKEN – Set #PPFC
Round Bottom – Pepsi 6"

1   2   3   4

Brutus (1982-1933) . . . . 1( )3   Popeye (1982-1929) . . . . 3( )3
Olive Oyl (1982-1919) . . . . 2( )3   Swee' Pea (1982-1933) . . . . 4( )3

PEPSI – Set #PRAC
Reproduction Add's Circa 1900
S.S. Hvy. Base – 5 9/16"

1   2   3   4

116

| After a Hard Game | . . . . | 1( )2 | Down on the Beach | . . . . | 3( )2 |
| Barney Oldfield | . . . . | 2( )2 | Drink at the Fountain | . . . . | 4( )2 |

RINGLING BROS. – Set #PCRB
(1975) 16 oz. Thin 6¼"

1-7

2-8

3-9

4-10

5-11

6-12

	NO "F"	With "F"
100th Anniversary	1( )3	7( )4
Bears That Dance	2( )3	8( )4
Combined Circus	3( )3	9( )4
Felix	4( )3	10( )4
The Greatest Show on Earth . . .	5( )3	11( )4
World's Biggest Menagerie	6( )3	12( )4

Note: The "F" is found on the bottom of the glass in a small shield. The "F" is for Federal Glass Company.

NORMAN ROCKWELL – Set #PNRF
Pepsi 5⅝" Ind Base – Scene on Frosted Sq.

3-7   4-8

	U.S.	Canadian
Beguiling Buttercup – 1949	1( )4	5( )4
Pride of Parenthood – 1958 . . .	2( )4	6( )4
Scholarly Pace – 1949	3( )4	7( )4
Young Mans Fancy – 1954	4( )4	8( )4

NORMAN ROCKWELL – Set #PNRA
(1979) S.O.R. Glass – Arby's and Pepsi

| 1 | 2 | 3 | 4 |

A Boy Meets His Dog 1 of 4	1( )2		Chilling Chore 3 of 4	3( )2
Downhill Daring 2 of 4	2( )2		Snow Sculpturing 4 of 4	4( )2

SPORTS COLLECTOR SERIES – Set #PSCS
(1979) Tail S.O.R. Glass – 5³⁄₈"

| 1 | 2 | 4 | 5 |

| 6 | 7 | 8 | 9 |

	1979	1980 Las Vegas
Backlash (Fishing)	1( )3	
Birdie (Golfer)	2( )2	11( )4
Heads Up (Soccer)	3( )3	
Leader of the Pack (Biker)	4( )2	12( )4
Line Drive (Baseball)	5( )2	13( )4
Nice Try (Racquetball)	6( )2	14( )4
Panic (Tennis Player) Woman . .	7( )2	15( )4
Psyche-Out (Skier)	8( )3	16( )4
Sportsmanship (Tennis Man) . . .	9( )3	
The Split (Bowling)	10( )4	

SUPER ACTION SERIES – Set #PSAB
(1981) Pepsi 5⅝" – Straight Side, Ind. Btm.

| | 6 | 1 | 5 | | 3 | 2 | 4 |

Dave Parker	1( )4	Mike Schmidt	4( )4
George Brett	2( )4	Reggie Jackson	5( )4
Jim Rice	3( )4	Tom Seaver	6( )4

SUPER HEROS – Set #PSHC
(1978) D.C. Comics – Brockway Glass Co. – Action

1-2

3

4

5

6

7-16

8

9

10

11

12

13

14

		6 5/16" 16 oz. Thick	6" Rd. Bottom	
Aquaman (1978)		1( )2		
Aquaman (No Date)		2( )10		
Batman (1966)		3( )2	9( )4	
Flash (1971)		4( )2	10( )4	
Robin (1978)		5( )2	11( )4	
Shazam (1978)		6( )2	12( )4	
Superman (1975)		7( )2	13( )4	
Wonder Woman (1978)		8( )2	14( )4	

Variations

Supergirl – D.C. Comic	15( )4	
Superman (1975) type no date or D.C. Comic . .	16( )4	
Wonder Woman – front logo	17( )4	

SUPER HEROS – Set #PSHM
Moon Behind Figures 16 oz. Thick
Brockway Glass Co. – 6 5/16" (1976)

1-15

2-16

3-17

4-18

5-19

6-20

7-21

8-22

9-23

10-24

11-25

12-26

13-27-29

14-28

	D.C.	N.P.P.
Aquaman	1( )5	15( )2
Batgirl	2( )3	16( )3
Batman	3( )3	17( )3
Flash	4( )3	18( )3
Green Arrow	5( )5	19( )4
Green Lantern	6( )6	20( )4
Joker	7( )6	21( )3
Penguin	8( )5	22( )3
Riddler	9( )4	23( )3
Robin	10( )3	24( )2
Shazam	11( )3	25( )2
Supergirl	12( )3	26( )4
Superman	13( )3	27( )3
Wonder Woman	14( )3	28( )2
Superman, no date or D.C. or N.P. Variation		29( )4

D.C. – D.C. Comics   N.P.P. – National Periodical Publications

SUPER HERO – Set #PSHD
Action, thick bottom glass – S.S.
Pepsi logo on two sides 5½"

1   2   3   4

Batman/Superman	1(	)4
Robin/Superman	2(	)4
Superman/Superman	3(	)7
Wonder Woman/Superman	4(	)4

SUPERMAN – Set #PSTM
The Movie (1979) – Ind. Btm.

1   2   3   4

5   6

From Kal-El (Child to Man of Steel)	1(	)2
Kal-El Comes To Earth	2(	)2
Lois Lane is Saved	3(	)2
Superman Saves The Day	4(	)2
The Caped Wonder To The Rescue	5(	)2
The Characters	6(	)2

WARNER BROS. – Set #PWBB

(1973) Brockway Glass Co. – 18 Different Characters

1   2   3   4

5   6   7   8

9   10   11   12

13   14   15   16

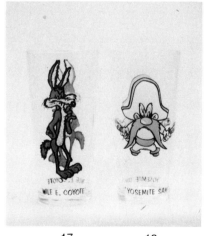

17   18

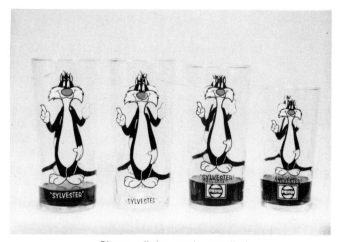

Shows all the way's supplied

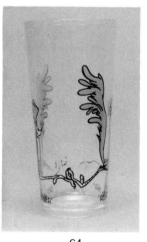

64

Price	Code	6 5/16" 16 oz. Thick Glass		6 5/16" 16 oz. LUN (4)	6 5/16" 16 oz. LUN (3)	5 1/8" 12 oz. LOS (4)
		(2)	(1)			
Beaky Buzzard		1WL( )	18BL( )			
Bugs Bunny		2WL( )	19BL( )	37BL( )	43BL( )	49BL( )
Cool Cat		3WL( )	20BL( )			
Daffy Duck		4WL( )	21BL( )	38BL( )	44BL( )	50BL( )
Elmer Fudd		5WL( )	22BL( )			
Foghorn Leghorn		6WL( )	23BL( )			

Henery Hawk	* 7WL( )	24BL( )			
Pepe Le Pew	* 8WL( )	25BL( )			
Clear Eyes		*26BL( )			
Petunia Pig	* 9WL( )				
Clear Eyes		27BL( )			
Porky Pig	10WL( )	28BL( )	39BL( )	45BL( )	51BL( )
Road Runner	11WL( )	29BL( )	40BL( )	46BL( )	52BL( )
Slow Poke					
Rodriguez	*12WL( )	30BL( )			
Speedy Gonzales	13WL( )	31BL( )			
Sylvester	14WL( )	32BL( )	41BL( )	47BL( )	
Tasmanian Devil	*15WL( )	33BL( )			
Tweety	16WL( )	34BL( )	42BL( )	48BL( )	53BL( )
Wile E Coyote	17WL( )	35BL( )			
Yosemite Sam	18WL( )	36BL( )			

VARIATIONS

Cool Cat– squinting	54WL( )3	Road Runner – no beep beep	62BL( )3
Cool Cat – orange and black dots halo' . . .	55BL( )3	Road Runner – no Warner Bros.	63BL( )3
Elmer Fudd – No. Warner Bros	56BL( )3	Road Runner – feet touch	64BL( )3
Foghorn – No. Warner Bros	57BL( )3	Speedy Gonzales – logo yellow	65BL( )3
Henery Hawk – logo yellow like body'	58BL( )3	Sylvester – no Warner Bros	66BL( )3
Pepe'Le Pew – no Warner Bros.	59BL( )3	Sylvester – small red nose	67BL( )3
Petunia Pig – logo, blue like dress	60BL( )3	Tweety – no Warner Bros	68BL( )3
Road Runner – clear eyes	61BL( )3	Yosemite Same – orange and black dots face .	69BL( )3

* The ones marked with an asterisk most difficult to find.

WL – White Lettering   BL – Black Lettering

LUN – Logo under name   LOS – Logo on side

WARNER BROS. – Set #PWBF

(1973) Federal Glass Co. – 18 Different Characters

	6¼" 16 oz. Thin		6 1/16" 15 oz. Thin LUN	5⅛" 12 oz. LUN
Price Code	(2)	(3)	(3)	(4)
Beaky Buzzard	1WL( )	20BL( )	39BL( )	
Bugs Bunny	2WL( )	21BL( )	40BL( )	57BL( )
Cool Cat	* 3WL( )	22BL( )	41BL( )	
Daffy Duck	4WL( )	23BL( )	42BL( )	58BL( )
Elmer Fudd	5WL( )	24BL( )	43BL( )	
Foghorn Leghorn	* 6WL( )	25BL( )	44BL( )	
Henery Hawk	* 7WL( )	26BL( )	45BL( )	
Pepe Le Pew (clear eyes)	8WL( )	27BL( )	46BL( )	
Petunia Pig (painted eyes)	9WL( )	28BL( )	47BL( )	
(clear eyes)	10WL( )	29BL( )		
Porky Pig	11WL( )	30BL( )	48BL( )	59BL( )
Road Runner	12WL( )	31BL( )	49BL( )	60BL( )
Slow Poke Rodriguez	*13WL( )	32BL( )	*50BL( )	
Speedy Gonzales	14WL( )	33BL( )	51BL( )	
Sylvester	15WL( )	34BL( )	52BL( )	61BL( )
Tasmanian Devil	16WL( )	35BL( )	*53BL( )	
Tweety	17WL( )	36BL( )	54BL( )	62BL( )
Wile E Coyote	18WL( )	37BL( )	55BL( )	
Yosemite Sam	19WL( )	38BL( )	56BL( )	

* The ones marked with an asterisk are most difficult to find.

NOTE: These glasses were produced by the Federal Glass Company. They have a very thin wall break easily and therefore command a premium price.

Warner Bros. – Set #PWBA
(1976) Action Series – 24 Different Glasses
Brockway Glass Co.

2   4   1   3

10   6   5   8

9   12   7   11

13   15   22   16

14   24   21   19

23   17   20   18

Beaky Buzzard/Cool Cat/Kite . . . . 1( )1
Elmer Fudd/Bugs/Shotgun/Carrots . . . . 2( )1
Henery Hawk/Tennis/Foghorn/Bomb . . . 3( )1
Pepe Le Pew/Kinked Hose/Daff . . . . 4( )1
Petunia Pig/Porky/Painting/Lawnmower . . . . . 5( )1
Road Runner/Catapult/Wile/Tunnel . . . . . . 6( )1
Sylvester/Tweety/Sawing Limb . . . . 7( )1
Tasmanian Devil/Daffy/Firecracker . . . . 8( )1
Tasmanian Devil/Porky/Fishing . . . . 9( )1
Tweety/Sylvester/Net/Bulldog . . . . 10( )1
Yosemite Sam/Bugs/Pirate/Cannon . . . . . . 11( )2
Yosemite Sam/Speedy/Gold Panning . . . . . 12( )2

Bugs Bunny/Mirror/Ray Gun/Martian . . . . 13( )6
Cool Cat/Coconut/Hunter . . . . 14( )5
Daffy Duck/Elmer/Bugs/Hunting Sign . . . . . . 15( )5
Elmer Fudd/Daffy/Band . . . . 16( )5
Foghorn Leghorn/Doghouse/Bomb . . . . 17( )5
Pepe Le Pew/Car/Perfume . . . . 18( )6
Porky Pig/Daffy/Pot/Ladle . . . . 19( )5
Slow Poke Rodriguez/Speedy/Hammer . . . . . 20( )5
Sylvester/Granny/Tweety/Birdbath . . . . 21( )5
Sylvester/Hoppy/Sylvester Jr./Boxing . . . . . 22( )5
Wile E Coyote/Road Runner/Skateboard . . . 23( )6
Wile E Coyote/Sheep Dog/Rope . . . . 24( )6

The last 12 scenes were special run only and were never produced in large volume.

VARIATIONS

Beaky/Cool Cat/Kite – blk. dots on cat's chest . 25( )3
Elmer/Bugs/Gun/Carrots – red dots on Elmer's face . 26( )3
Pepe/Hose/Daffy/Kiwk – no 1976 Warner Bros. . 27( )3
Petunia/Painting/Porky/Mowing – clear last note . 28( )3

Road Runner/Catapult/Wile/Tunnel –
no Warner Bros. . . . . 29( )3
Sylvester/Limb/Tweety/Sawing –
no Warner Bros. 1976 . . . . 30( )3

WARNER BROS. – Set #PWBR
(1979) Action Series – Looney Tunes
5⁷⁄₈" Rd. Btm.

1

2

3

4

5

6

Bugs Bunny/Daffy Duck . . . . 1( )1
Daffy Duck/Bugs Bunny . . . . 2( )1
Porky Pig/Bugs Bunny . . . . 3( )1
Road Runner/Wile E Coyote . . . . 4( )1
Sylvester/Tweety . . . . 5( )1
Tweety/Sylvester . . . . 6( )1

WARNER BROS. – Set #PWBS
(Star) Looney Tunes – 5⅞" – Rd. Btm.

1

2

3

4

5

6

7

Bugs Bunny (1966) . . . . 1( )2	Sylvester (1966) . . . . 5( )2
Daffy Duck (1980) . . . . 2( )2	Tweety (1966) . . . . 6( )2
Porky Pig (1966) . . . . 3( )2	Yosemite Sam (1966) . . . . 7( )3
Road Runner (1966) . . . . 4( )2	

NOTE: The dates after the character name indicates copyright information and not the date the glass was released.

WARNER BROS. – Set #PWBC
Canadian Series – 10 oz. thin 4¾"

	1975	1977	1978
Bugs Bunny	1( )3	7( )3	13( )3
Daffy Duck	2( )3	8( )3	14( )3
Porky Pig	3( )3	9( )3	15( )3
Road Runner	4( )3	10( )3	16( )3
Sylvester	5( )3	11( )3	17( )3
Tweety	6( )3	12( )3	18( )3

WARNER BROS. – Set #PWBH
Canadian Series 4¾" – Tim Horton Donut Shops

5	4	2

Elmer Fudd (1978) . . . . 1(   )4
Foghorn Ledhorn (1978) . . . . 2(   )4
Pepe Le Pew (1978) . . . . 3(   )4

1	6

Speedy Gonzales (1978) . . . . 4(   )4
Wile E Coyote (1978) . . . . 5(   )4
Yosemite Sam (1978) . . . . 6(   )4

WISCONSIN BADGER SERIES – Set #PWBG

4	6	7	9

	81-82		79-80	
	No Logo Brockway	Rd. Btm. Pepsi	Rd. Btm. Mt. Dew	Brockway Pepsi
Baseball				4( )5
Basketball				5( )5
Football				6( )5
Hockey	1( )	2( )	3( )	7( )5
Track				8( )5
Wrestling				9( )5

PEPSI MISCELLANEOUS – Set #PCMX

3	1	5	15

7

9

25   17   35

23   21   19

27

29

38

39

41

47

43 front

43 back

49

51

55

57

58

30

63

65

89   69   67

130

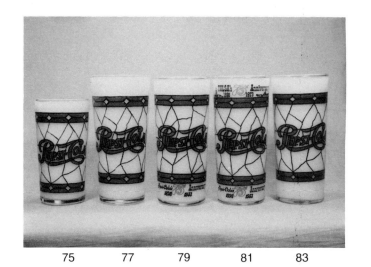

73   75   77   79   81   83   85

PENGUINS – Set #PEN
Elby's Big Boy

Mario Lemieux #66 . . . . 1(   )1
Paul Coffey #66 . . . . 1(   )1
Rob Brown #44 . . . . 3(   )1
Zarley Zalapski #33 . . . . 4(   )1

PIERRE THE BEAR – Set #PTB
LK's

| 1 | 2 | 6 | 7 |

Fall . . . . 1(   )2   5(   )2
Spring . . . . 2(   )2   6(   )2
Summer . . . . 3(   )2   7(   )2
Winter . . . . 4(   )2   8(   )2

PITTSBURGH PIRATES – Set #PPE
(Coca Cola) Elby's 6" flare top – creased btm.
Released in 1988

4   3   1

Bobby Bonilla, Doug Drabek . . . . 1(   )2
Jim Gott, Jose Lind . . . . 2(   )2
Mike Dunne, Andy Van Slyke . . . . 3(   )2
Mike Lavalliere, Barry Bonos . . . . 4(   )2

PITTSBURGH STEELERS – Set PTS
(1976) 6¼" NFL, MSA

10   11

Bleier, Rockey #20	1(	)3
Blount, Mel #47	2(	)3
Bradshaw, Terry #12	3(	)3
Edwards, Glen #27	4(	)3
Greene, Joe #75	5(	)3
Ham, Jack #59	6(	)3
Lambert, Jack #58	7(	)3
Mansfield, Ray #56	8(	)3
Russell, Andy #34	10(	)3
White, Dwight #78	11(	)3

PIZZA PETE – Set #PIZ
6" Seattle Washington

Boom Boom Mushroom	1(	)3	Olive-Name Me!	4(	)3
Charlie Cheezerella	2(	)3	Pizza Pete	5(	)3
Frankie Pepperoni	3(	)3	Rosie Tomato	6(	)3

PIZZA TIME THEATRE – Set #PIT
5⅝" Action Libbey Glass Co. – Ind. Btm.

2   3   4   1

Chuck E Cheese	1(	)2
Jasper T Jowles	2(	)2
Mr. Munch	3(	)2
Pasqually	4(	)2

PIZZA HUT – Set #PCB
CB Series Springfield Missouri
P.A.T. Ward – Leonardo TTV – Pizza Hut
Brockway Glass Co.

1   3   4

2   6   5

16oz. Thick

Bullwinkle (blue express truck) . . . . 1( )6	
Bullwinkle (fishing pole, rocky underwater) . . . 2( )6	
Bullwinkle (in police car) . . . . 3( )6	
Bullwinkle (rocky in tree, green truck) . . . . . . 4( )6	

Dudley Do-Right (in helicopter
 over Boris red truck) . . . . 5( )6
Underdog (holding CB mike,
 flying over crashed cars) . . . . 6( )6

POPEYE'S FAMOUS FRIED CHICKEN – Set #PFC
5⅞" creased and indented base

BRUTUS OLIVE OYL POPEYE SWEE'PEA

1   2   3   4

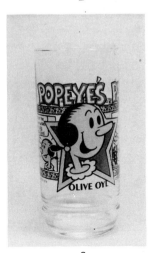

BRUTUS OLIVE OYL POPEYE SWEE'PEA

5   6   7   8

		1978	1979				
		Sports	Pals				
Brutus		1( )2	5( )2	Popeye		3( )2	7( )2
Olive Oyl		2( )2	6( )2	Swee' Pea		4( )2	8( )2

POPEYE'S KOLLECT-A-SET – Set #PKS
(1975) Coca Cola 5⅞" with a ¾" ind. base

1

2

3

4

5

6

7

8

Brutus	1( ) 1	Popeye	5( ) 1
Castor Oil	2( )10 +	Rough House	6( ) 0
Geezil	3( )10 +	Swee Pea	7( ) 0
Olive Oyl	4( ) 1	Wimpy	8( ) 0

POPEYE – Set #POY
(1933) King Feature Syndicate 4⅝"
Early 30's Issue – Two Color

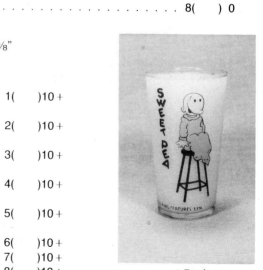

4-Front

Popeye Boxing, Olive Oyl admiring
pink, blue, (1919-29) . . . . 1( )10 +
Popeye smoking pipe, Goon
blue, yellow (1929) . . . . 2( )10 +
Popeye smoking with hand extended,
Oscar, orange, yellow (1929) . . . . 3( )10 +
Popeye smoking with hand extended,
Swee'Pea, green, yellow (1929) . . . . . 4( )10 +
Popeye standing hand on chin, no hat
Jeep, yellow, red (1929-36) . . . . 5( )10 +
Popeye smoking pipe, Wimpy,
blue, black (1929) . . . . 6( )10 +
Popeye, Sea Hag . . . . 7( )10 +
Popeye, Bluto . . . . 8( )10 +

4-Back

POPPLES – Set #POP
Kid from Cleveland, No logo – Pizza Hut
5⅞" (1986) Rd. Btm.

1	2	3	4

Party Popple . . . . 1( )1   Puffball Popple . . . . 3( )1
PC Popple . . . . 2( )1   Puzzle Popple . . . . 4( )1

PORTLAND OREGON TRAILBLAZERS – Set #POT
MBA Basketball – Sunshine Pizza Exchange
5⅝" S.S. Ind. Base (1983-84)

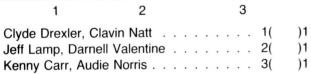

1	2	3

Clyde Drexler, Clavin Natt . . . . 1( )1   Mychael Thompson, Peter Verhoevan . . . 4( )1
Jeff Lamp, Darnell Valentine . . . . 2( )1   Wayne Cooper, Tom Piotrowski . . . . . . 5( )1
Kenny Carr, Audie Norris . . . . 3( )1   Lafayette Lever, Jim Paxson . . . . 6( )1

PORTLAND PLAYERS – Set #PPO
Oregon NBA – R.C. Cola (1979) 6¼"

| 1 | 2 | 4 | | 5 | 6 | 8 |

Bill Walton . . . . 1( )3				Larry Steele . . . . 5( )3		
Bob Gross . . . . 2( )3				Lionel Hollins . . . . 6( )3		
Dave Twardzik . . . . 3( )3				Lloyd Neal . . . . 7( )3		
Johnny Davis . . . . 4( )3				Maurice Lucas . . . . 8( )3		

RAGGEDY ANN AND ANDY – Set #RAA
Bobbs Merrill Co. 6" – S.S. Creased Btm.

Doing Chores . . . . 1( )1
Gone Fishing . . . . 2( )1
Raggedy Roller . . . . 3( )1

RAISINS – Set #RAI
The California – Applause Lic. (1989) Calrab
All glasses have the same wrap around scene of dancing and singing raisins

1-6

4"	1(	)1
5 5/16" S.S. Thin	2(	)1
5 3/16" Creased than ind. base	3(	)1
6⅞" Ice Tea Glass, Comes in at BTM	4(	)1
6 7/16" Decanter with Lid S.S.	5(	)1
Juice Jar and Lid	6(	)1

RED BARON PIZZA – Set #RBP
Mail Offer (1984)

Curtiss Atlantic Flying Boat . . . . 1( )2			Sopworth Camel . . . . 3( )2	
Fokker Dri . . . . 2( )2			Wright Flyer . . . . 4( )2	

THE RED STEER RESTAURANT – Set #RSR
(1976) Bi-Cen. 5⅞"

Boise, Idaho Issue	1( )2		Ginkgo Petrfied, Washington Issue	10( )2
Cataldo Mission, Idaho Issue	2( )2		Fort Okanogan, Washington Issue	11( )2
Fort Hall, Idaho Issue	3( )2		Fort Simcoe, Washington Issue	12( )2
Idaho City, Idaho Issue	4( )2		Lewis and Clark Trail, Washington Issue	13( )2
Lewis and Clark, Idaho Issue	5( )2		Olympia, Washington Issue	14( )2
Massacre Rocks, Idaho Issue	6( )2		Walla Walla, Colville, Washington Wagon Trail	
Oregon Trail, Idaho Issue	7( )2		Washington	15( )2
Silver City, Idaho Issue	8( )2		Whitman Mission, Washington Issue	16( )2
Conconully, Washington Issue	9( )2			

RETURN OF THE JEDI – Set #ROJ
Star Wars (1983) Burger King – 5⅝" Rd.

1	2	3	4

Ewok	1( )1	Jabba	3( )1
Han Solo	2( )1	Luke Skywalker	4( )1

RINGLING BRO'S AND BARNUM BAILY CIRCUS –
Set #RIN
6" Rd. Btm.

Marching Clown with Baton, blue	1( )2
Dancing Clown with Tambourine, green	2( )2
Clown Walking Dog with large Chain for Leash, yellow	3( )2
Clown taking a Shower, Bath in a Tub on Wheels, red	4( )2
Clown walking with a small Umbrella, green	5( )2
Clown riding on a small car, yellow	6( )2
Clown carrying a stuffed Lion, red	7( )2
Clown with a small Megaphone and a Plumger, blue	8( )2

7

ROBIN HOOD AND FRIENDS – Set #RHC
Canadian – Fed. Glass 4⅝" Taper Down
Number in hat on back

Robin Hood	1( )3	Maid Marian	5( )3
King Richard	2( )3	Will Scarlett	6( )3
Frair Tuck	3( )3	Prince John	7( )3
Little John	4( )3	Sheriff of Nottingham	8( )3

ROBIN HOOD – Set #RHX
Miscellaneous

3

5⅛" Robin Hood Meets Little John around
Rim them Josting . . . . 1( )2
6⅜" Brockway Style Glass, Robin Hood Twice – below rim,
no logo's – Robin Hood, Frair Tuck, Little John . 2( )2
5" Robin Hood and His Merry Men, green, brown . 3( )2

NORMAN ROCKWELL

NORMAN ROCKWELL – Set #RAS
The Americana Series – Saturday Evening Post Covers

1   2   3   4

1 of 4 – October 21, 1950 – 96771 . . . . 1( )1
2 of 4 – (1935) Calendar – 96771 . . . . 2( )1
3 of 4 – April, 27, 1935 – 96771 . . . . 3( )1
4 of 4 – April 29, 1939 – 96771 . . . . 4( )1

NORMAN ROCKWELL – Set #RRP
Reproductions of Original Paintings – Coca Cola
No Date

2   3   4

Boy at Tree Eating . . . . 1(   )1
Boy at Well . . . . 2(   )1

Boy Fishing, Dog Watching Cork . . . . 3(   )1
Boy Sitting at Water, Coke in hand . . . . . . 4(   )1

NORMAN ROCKWELL SATURDAY EVENING POST
Set #RSE
Santa – Coca Cola

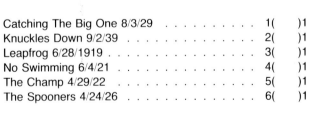

12/4/26 Santa Globe . . . . 1(   )1
12/2/22 Santa Doll House . . . . 2(   )1
12/4/20 Santa Book . . . . 3(   )1

1   2   3

NORMAN ROCKWELL – Set #REP
Saturday Evening Post

1   2   3   4

5   6

Catching The Big One 8/3/29 . . . . 1(   )1
Knuckles Down 9/2/39 . . . . 2(   )1
Leapfrog 6/28/1919 . . . . 3(   )1
No Swimming 6/4/21 . . . . 4(   )1
The Champ 4/29/22 . . . . 5(   )1
The Spooners 4/24/26 . . . . 6(   )1

NORMAN ROCKWELL – Set #RPC
Saturday Evening Post Covers – Pedestal
Coca Cola – Ped. Base

1

2

3

4

Box they came in

After The Prom 5-25-57 . . . . 1(　)1
Old Friend at Trails End 10/28 . . . . 2(　)1
Sunstruck 7-13-40 . . . . 3(　)1
Washington at Valley Forge 2/23/35 . . . . 4(　)1

NORMAN ROCKWELL SUMMER SCENES – Set #RSA
(1987) Arby's 6¼" Saturday Evening Post Covers

2　　　　3　　　　4

Gone Fishing . . . . 1(　)1
Gramps at the Plate . . . . 2(　)1
No Swimming . . . . 3(　)1
Sunset . . . . 4(　)1

NORMAN ROCKWELL – Set #ROS
Outdoor Scenes Coca Cola

Buttered Corn . . . . 1(　)1
Different Foods . . . . 2(　)1
Smiling Face . . . . 3(　)1
White Flower . . . . 4(　)1

RODEO WORLD CHAMPION SERIES – Set #RWC

Bobby Berger . . . . 1(   )10
Bruce Ford . . . . 2(   )10
Carol Goostree . . . . 3(   )10

Don Gray . . . . 4(   )10
Paul Tierney . . . . 5(   )10
Stan Williamson . . . . 6(   )10

ROOT BEAR – Set #ROT
A & W The Great

1   3   2

The Great Root Bear – 16oz. Brockway . . . . . 1(   )2
The Great Root Bear – Back To You
   S.S. Ind. Base . . . . 2(   )2
Pitcher Showing Bear . . . . 3(   )5

H SALT – Set #SLT
Brockway Glass Co.

1

2

3

4

5   6

Chinese Lorcha . . . . 1(   )5
James Watt . . . . 2(   )5
The Caravel "Nina" . . . . 3(   )5
The Flying Cloud . . . . 4(   )5
The Frigate . . . . 5(   )5
The Prince Royal (1610) . . . . 6(   )5

SEARCH FOR SPOCK – STAR TREK III – Set #SFS
Taco Bell (1984) Double Creased – 5⅝"

1	2	3	4

Enterprise Destroyed . . . . 1(　)1
Fal Tor Pan . . . . 2(　)1
Lord Kruge . . . . 3(　)1
Spock Lives . . . . 4(　)1

SEATTLE SUPERSONICS – Set #SAS
Godfather's Pizza – Rd. Btm. 5⅝" – NBA

1　　2　　3　　4

Thompson, Vranes, Donaldson . . . . 1(　)1
Williams, Wilkins, Skirms . . . . 2(　)1
Smith, Brown, Radford . . . . 3(　)1
Kelser, Shelton, Talbert . . . . 4(　)1

SEVEN-UP (7 UP) MISCELLANEOUS – Set #SVX
Soda Glasses

1	2	3	10

7Up – Dark green dbl. crease – 3⅞"	1( )2		Large 7Up Vertical 6½" Ped. Base	6( )1
7Up Uncola – upside down – 5⅞" Glass . . .	2( )1		Lil' Un – 3" Cut off soda glass	7( )1
Lady in Swim Suit Kicking – 7Up logo – 5 9/16".	3( )1		Look Who's Turning Diet 7Up – 6 9/16" Thin . .	8( )1
Large 7Up Horizontial – Goblet – Green 6" . . .	4( )1		Seven Up in white script 5⅜" – 4 ribs at btm . .	9( )1
Large 7Up Vertical 5¼" Tumbler	5( )1		Seven-Up Vertical Green Letters, .2 ltr Glass . .	10( )1

SHIRT TALES – Set #SHT
By Hallmark

1		3	2

3⅜" Flared Rim	1( )1	9" Flared Rim	4( )1
5⅜" Flared Rim	2( )1	3⅜" Flared Rim, Char. only green shrubes . . .	5( )1
6" Flared Rim	3( )1		

SMURF – Set #SMU
(1982) Rd. Btm. 6"

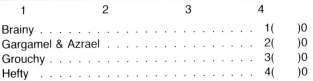

1	2	3	4	5	6	7	8

Brainy	1( )0	Jokey	5( )0
Gargamel & Azrael	2( )0	Lazy	6( )0
Grouchy	3( )0	Papa	7( )0
Hefty	4( )0	Smurfette	8( )0

SMURF – Set #SMR
(1983) Rd. Btm. 6"

1	2	3

Baker Smurf . . . . 1( )0
Clumsy Smurf . . . . 2( )0
Handy Smurf . . . . 3( )0

4	5	6

Harmony Smurf . . . . 4( )0
Papa Smurf . . . . 5( )0
Smurfette . . . . 6( )0

SPARKIE BOY GLASSES – Set #SPR
G.P.G. Company, Cincinnati Ohio – Copyright ASE

1	3	4	5

6	7	8	Side of glass

Back of glass

Sparkie/Drum	1( )3
Sparkie/Piano	2( )3
Sparkie/Playing Glasses	3( )3
Sparkie/Saxophone	4( )3
Sparkie/Trombone	5( )3
Sparkie/Trumpet	6( )3
Sparkie/Ukulele	7( )3
Sparkie/Xylophone	8( )3

SPOKAN DAILY CHRONICLE – Set #SPC
Spokesman Review 5½" Ped. Base

Kidnapped Suspect is Indited	1( )1	Fire Tonight Licking Up	3( )1
Lusitania Carrying 2067 Soul's	2( )1	Apollo Pair Finishes Historic Walk	4( )1

STAR WARS – Set #STW
(1977) Burger King 5⅝"

1	2	3	4

Chewbacca	1( )1	Luke Skywalker	3( )1
Darth Vader	2( )1	R-2, D-2	4( )1

STAR TREK – Set #STM
The Motion Picture – Coca Cola (1980) 5⅝"

1	2	3

Enterprise	1(	)3
Ilia/Decker	2(	)3
Kirk/Spock/McCoy	3(	)3

STAR TREK – Set #STD
Dr. Pepper 6⅛" Glass

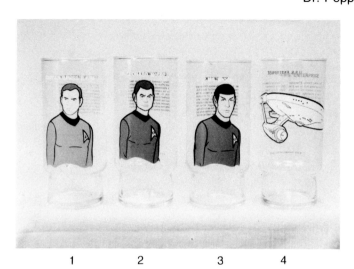

1   2   3   4   5   6

7   8

	1976		1978	
Capt. Kirk	1(	)3	5(	)4
Dr. McCoy	2(	)3	6(	)4
Mr. Spock	3(	)3	7(	)4
USS Enterprise	4(	)3	8(	)4

STRAWBERRY SHORTCAKE – Set #STS
American Greetings Corp. (1980) Barrel Shape

"It's The Berries" (1980)	1(	)1
"Strawberry Shortcake" (1980)	2(	)1
"There's More Where This Came From" (1980) .	3(	)1

1   3

SUBWAY LIMITED – Set #SUL
(Christmas) 5⁷⁄₈" Rd. Btm.
Carol by Charles Dickens

Bob Cratchit . . . . 1(   )2
Edenezer Scrooge . . . . 2(   )2
Tiny Tim & Bob Cratchit . . . . 3(   )2
Ghost of Past & Present . . . . 4(   )2

3   2   1   4

SUNDAY FUNNIES – Set #SUN
Libbey Glass Co. 5⁵⁄₈"

1   2   3   4

5   6   7

Brenda Starr (1976) NY Times . . . . 1(   ) 2
Broom Hilda (1976) Chicago Times . . . . . 2(   )10 +
Gasoline Alley (1976) Chicago Times . . . . . 3(   ) 2
Little Orphan Annie (1976) NY Times . . . . 4(   ) 2

Moon Mullins (1976) NY Times . . . . 5(   ) 2
Smilin' Jack (1976) NY Times . . . . 6(   ) 2
Terry and The Pirates
 (1976) News Synd. Co., Inc . . . . 7(   ) 2

SUPER MARIO 2 – Set #SMB
By Nintendo (1989)

1-4

5¼" Tin Tumbler	1( )0
6¼" Tumbler	2( )0
8" Super Mug	3( )0
7" Cookie Jar	4( )0

SUPERMAN ACTION – Set #SUP
(1964) National Periodical – Jelly Glass

1-7

3 view of #6

9

	4¼"	5¾"
Superman in Action	1( )5	7( )6
Superman Finds Spaceship	2( )5	8( )6
Superman To The Rescue	3( )5	9( )6
Superman Uses X-Ray Vision	4( )5	10( )6
Superman Fighting The Dragon . . .	5( )5	11( )6
Clark Kent Changes To Superman . .	6( )5	12( )6

Each glass comes in two different color combinations, they are, orange top, lt. blue btm.; red top, gray btm.; pink top, turquoise btm.; turquoise top, orange btm.; gray top, red btm.; and orange top, blue btm.

Superman, DC Comics (1971)
  short hvy. base – flying . . . . 9(   )6
Superman, DC Comics (1978)
  5 9/16" – Breaking Chains . . . . 10(   )6

TACO MAYO – Set #TAM
(Coca Cola)

1

Mousecat . . . . 1(   )2

TACO VILLA – Set #TAV
(1977) Character – Libbey Glass Co.
S.S. Ind. Base

| 1 | 2 | 8 | 3 |

| | | | | 4 | 5 | 6 | 7 |

Beauregard . . . . 1(   )5

Frawley . . . . 2(   )5

Irving . . . . 3(   )5

Julius . . . . 4(   )5

Lazlo . . . . 5(   )5

Mortimer . . . . 6(   )5

Sigmund . . . . 7(   )5

Harley . . . . 8(   )5

TACO VILLA – Set #TAC
(1979) Sport's – Libbey Glass Co.
5⅝" S.S. Ind. Base

| 1 | 2 | 3 | 7 |

| 5 | 8 | 4 | 6 |

Beauregard	1( )3	Julius, golf (no date)	5( )3
Frawley, skiing	2( )3	Lazlo, baseball	6( )3
Harley, football	3( )3	Mortimer, basketball	7( )3
Irving, tennis	4( )3	Sigmund, surfing	8( )3

TERRYTOONS INC. – Set #TER
(1940's) Federal Glass – 4¾" black & yellow

4   1

Sour Puss	1( )8
Dim Wits	2( )8
Terry Bears	3( )8
Dinkey	4( )8

TERRYTOONS – Set #TRR
(1977) 16oz. Thick

1

Mighty Mouse . . . . 1( )10 +

TEXAS UNDER FLAGS – Set #TUF
6½" Frosted Color – Late (1950's)

Anson Jones – U.S. Flag	1( )2	Hayden Edwards – Fredonian Rebellion Flag	6( )2
Cavelier Dela Salle – French Flag	2( )2	Stephen F. Austin – Mexican Flag	7( )2
Edwin W. Moore – Texas Navy Flag	3( )2	Pitcher	8( )3
Francisco Coronado – Spanish Flag	4( )2	Wooden Tray for Above	9( )3
Gen. Albert S. Johnson – Confederate Flag	5( )2		

THOUGHT FACTORY – Set #TFA
4⁵⁄₈" Arby's (1982) S.O.R. Glass – Hvy Base

1	2	3	4

Dedication . . . . 1(   )1
First Flake . . . . 2(   )1

Luck Out . . . . 3(   )1
Pool Shark . . . . 4(   )1

CHICAGO TRIBUNE – Set #DTG
Dominos Pizza – 16oz. Brockway

1

Dick Tracy . . . . 1(   )10 +

DICK TRACY – Set #DTC
Character Glasses – 5" Frosted hvy base (1960's)

B.O. Plenty . . . . 1( )5		Shakey . . . . 5( )5
Breathless Mahoney . . . . 2( )5		Snowflake . . . . 6( )5
Dick Tracy . . . . 3( )5		Tess Truehart . . . . 7( )5
Gravel Gertie . . . . 4( )5		Vitamin Flintheart . . . . 8( )5

TRIVIAL PURSUIT – Set #TRI
4⅛" Frosted Panels

4

Art & Literature	. . . .	1(	)2
Entertainment	. . . .	2(	)2
Geography	. . . .	3(	)2
History	. . . .	4(	)2
Science and Nature	. . . .	5(	)2
Sports and Leisure	. . . .	6(	)2

MARK TWAIN COUNTRY SERIES – Set #TMC
Burger King (1985) – Rd. 5"

Huck Finn	. . . .	1(	)2	Octagonial Study	. . . .	3(	)2
Mark Twain	. . . .	2(	)2	Tom Sawyer	. . . .	4(	)2

ULTRAMART – Set #ULT
(1986) Anchor Hocking

Chicken Eggstraordinary	. . . .	1(	)3	Car Wash / Pig	. . . .	4(	)3
Oily Bird	. . . .	2(	)3	Fillerup / Pup	. . . .	5(	)3
Ultra Moo / Cow	. . . .	3(	)3	2 Ft 3 Eagle	. . . .	6(	)3

UNIVERSAL MONSTER SERIES – Set #UNI
Straight Sides

Front of 1   Front of 3   Front of 5

Back of 1   Back of 3   Back of 5

6

7

8

9

	1980 5½"		1960's 6⅝"	
Creature from the Black Lagoon . . .	1(	)6	6(	)4
Wolfman	2(	)6	7(	)4
Frankenstein	3(	)6	8(	)4

Mummy	4(	)6	9(	)4
Mutant	5(	)6		
Dracula	6(	)6		

URCHINS – Set #URC
Coca Cola – Creased and Ind. Base – 5¾"

1

2

3

4

5

6

A Little Fun	1(	)2
Friends Make Life	2(	)2
Good Friends	3(	)2
Good Fun Is Par	4(	)2
Life Is Fun	5(	)2
Serve Up Sunshine	6(	)2

WARNER BROS. – Set #WBA
(1974) 8oz. Welches – 4¼"

1

2

3

4

5

6

7

8

Bugs Leads A Merry Chase . . . . 1(   )0
Foghorn Switches Henery's Egg . . . . 2(   )0
I Tawt I Taw A Puddy Tat . . . . 3(   )0
Speedy Snaps Up The Cheese . . . . 4(   )0

That's All Folks . . . . 5(   )0
Thufferin Thucatash . . . . 6(   )0
Whats Up Doc – Fresh Carrots . . . . 7(   )0
Wile E Heads For A Big Finish . . . . 8(   )0

WARNER BROS. – Set #WBC
(1976) 8 oz. Welches – 4¼"

1

2

3

4

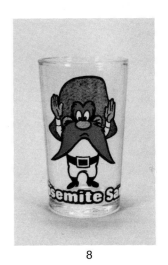

	5		6

Bugs Bunny	. . . .	1( )1
Daffy Duck	. . . .	2( )1
Elmer Fudd	. . . .	3( )1
Foghorn Leghorn	. . . .	4( )1
Porky Pig	. . . .	5( )1
Road Runner	. . . .	6( )1

7		8

Tweety	. . . .	7( )1
Yosemite Sam	. . . .	8( )1

Note: Faces in bottom of glass are tweety, sylvester, porky, bugs bunny, elmer, yosemite, blank. Eight times seven faces equals fifty-six glass to the set.

WARNER BROS. – Set #WAR
(1930's) 5" L.S.C.

Elmer	. . . .	1( )6
Fluffnums	. . . .	2( )6
Patrick Parrot	. . . .	3( )6
Petunia Pig	. . . .	4( )6
Porky Pig	. . . .	5( )6

4   2   3   1

Warner Bros. – Set #WBG
(1989) Canadian 3⅞"
Names Don't Appear on Glass

Bug's Bunny	. . . .	1( )2
Daffy Duck	. . . .	2( )2
Road Runner	. . . .	3( )2
Sylvester	. . . .	4( )2
Tweety	. . . .	5( )2
Wile E. Coyote	. . . .	6( )2

1–6

WELCHES – Set #WAN
AFC and NFC Team Names

3   4

AFC Eastern Division . . . . 1(   )1
AFC Central Division . . . . 2(   )1
AFC Western Division . . . . 3(   )1
NFC Eastern Division . . . . 4(   )1
NFC Central Division . . . . 5(   )1
NFC Western Division . . . . 6(   )1

WELCHES – Set #WEL
AFC and NFC Helmet's Glasses

1

American Football Conference . . . . 1(   )1
National Football Conference . . . . 2(   )1

WELCHES – Set #WLD
(1988) Dinosaurs 10oz. – 4" Tall

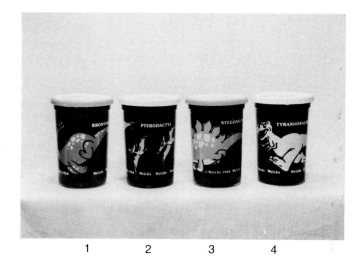

1   2   3   4

Brontosaurs . . . . 1(   )0
Pterodactyl . . . . 2(   )0
Stegosaurs . . . . 3(   )0
Tyrannosaurs Rex . . . . 4(   )0

WENDY'S – Set #WNX
Miscellaneous

1

2

Clara Peller "Where's The Beef" 5" & 5⅞" . . . . 1(　　)2
Wendy's (1982) World's Fair . . . . 2(　　)2

THE WIZARD OF ID SERIES – Set #WOI
Arby's Collector Series (1983)
Field Enterprise

1

2

3

4

5

6

Bung . . . . 1(　　)2
King . . . . 2(　　)2
Larson E Pettifogger . . . . 3(　　)2
Sir Rodney . . . . 4(　　)2
Spook . . . . 5(　　)2
Wizard . . . . 6(　　)2

WIZARD OF OZ

WIZARD OF OZ – Set #WKA
Kansas "Land of Ah's" 5⅝" Ind. Base S.S.
Colonel Sanders – Libbey Glass Co.

Front   1   Back

Tin Man	1(	)4
Scarecrow	2(	)4
Dorothy	3(	)4
Lion	4(	)4

WIZARD OF OZ – Set #WOK
Coca Cola, Krystal Rest. (1989) 6⅛"
Flare top – Libbey Glass Co.

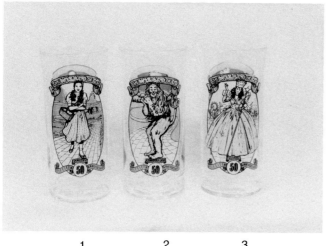

   1   2   3   4   5   6

Dorothy	1(	)2	Scarecrow	4(	)2
Cowerly Lion	2(	)2	Tin Man	5(	)2
Glinda	3(	)2	Wicked Witch of the West	6(	)2

WIZARD OF OZ – Set #WOZ
(1939) Copyright (1970's) Premium

1

Dorothy, Scarecrow, Tinman, Lion . . . . 1(   )10

WIZARD OF OZ – Set #WIZ
Swift Peanut Butter

1

2

3

4

5

6

7

8

9

10

11

12

13

14

15

17

18

	Wavy Btm.	Plain Btm.	Fluted Btm.
Woodsman	1( )3	7( )3	13( )3
Wizard	2( )3	8( )3	14( )3
Scarecrow	3( )3	9( )3	15( )3
Toto	4( )3	10( )3	16( )3
Lion	5( )3	11( )3	17( )3
Dorothy	6( )3	12( )3	18( )3

WIZARD OF OZ – Set #WOL
(1939) 4½" Loews Inc. – Thin glass, red ring around top

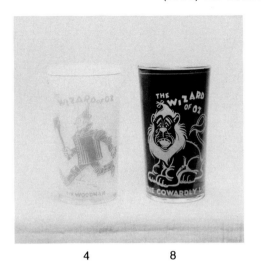

4   8

Bad Witch	. . . .	1(	)6
Dorothy	. . . .	2(	)6
Good Witch	. . . .	3(	)6
Lion	. . . .	4(	)6
Scarecrow	. . . .	5(	)6
Tin Woodsman	. . . .	6(	)6
Toto	. . . .	7(	)6
Wizard	. . . .	8(	)6

WIZARD OF OZ – Set #WMA
Fluted Base 5" S & Co. – Movie Action Characters

1   2   3   5

4   6

Emerald City	. . . .	1(	)4
Flying Monkeys	. . . .	2(	)4
Glinda	. . . .	3(	)4
Winkies	. . . .	4(	)4
Witch of the North	. . . .	5(	)4
Witch of the West	. . . .	6(	)4

WORLD WRESTLING FEDERATION – Set #WWF
Canadian 4 7/16" – Schwartz Peanut Butter

4   2   1   3

Hulkamania	. . . .	1(	)1
Jake The Snake	. . . .	2(	)1
Macho Madness	. . . .	3(	)1
Ultimate Warrior	. . . .	4(	)1

ZIGGY – Set #ZIG
(1977) 7Up Collector Series

1   2   3   4

On A Bike	. . . .	1(	)1	With Ducks	. . . .	3(	)1
On A Swing	. . . .	2(	)1	With Fishbowl	. . . .	4(	)1

ZIGGY – Set #ZIP
(1979) 5⅞" – Ind. Crease

1-5-9   2-6-10   3-7-11   4-8-12

	No Logo	Hardies	Pizza Inn
Be Nice To Little Things .	1( )1	5( )1	9( )1
Smile, It's Good For			
Your Complexion	2( )1	6( )1	10( )1

| Time For A Pizza Break . | 3( )1 | 7( )1 | 11( )1 |
| Try To Have A Nice Day . | 4( )1 | 8( )1 | 12( )1 |

ZIGGY – Set #ZGG
Universal Press S.O.R. Glass – 3³₈" Heavy Base

Your The One, Big #1 on glass . . . . 1( )2
Thats You, Big #2 on glass . . . . 2( )2
If Your Number, Big #3 on glass . . . . 3( )2

1   2   3

MISCELLANEOUS GLASSES AND SETS – Set #MGX

1   5   7   11

13   15   17   19

| 21 | 23 | 25 | 27 |

| 31 | 35 | 39 Glasses |

| 39 Box | 41 | 47 |

165

53

53 Side-View

53

55

59

61

63

69

71

73

77

81

87

93 Front

93 Back

95

97

102

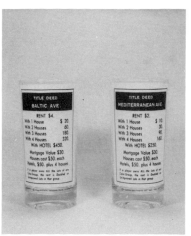

105

113

115

117

119

127

131

133

137

138

141

143

147

153   151   149

155

159

161

163

167

McCarthy, Charlie, Radio Premium AAFES . . 103(   )1
Mt. St. Helens (May 18, 1980) AAFES . . . . . 103(   )1
Monopoly Glass 5 9/16" Title Deed Baltic Ave . 105(   )1
Musical Instrument Glass – no logo – no date
   brown, yellow . . . . 107(   )1
Oklahoma University State Anniv.
   (1958) Bob Harrison #54 . . . . 109(   )1
Pacific Eight Conference – 8 logos
   College . . . . 111(   )2
Pizza Inn – Man Tossing Dough – 6" Heavy . 113(   )1
Rawlings -R5 Football 5¼" Hvy. Base S.S. . . 115(   )1
R.C. Blue Tiffany Design – R.C. in red circle . 117(   )1
R.C. Salutes the Champs
   (NBA) Portland Players . . . . 119(   )1
Ringo – 4¾" Nems Enterprises (1964) . . . . . 121(   )10
Ringo – 5½" Musical Notes, Records
   & Guitar (1966) . . . . 123(   )10
Round Table Pizza Glass "Wizard"
   flare/crease . . . . 125(   )1
Shakey's 20th Anniversary – red and yellow
   leaded window design . . . . 127(   )2
Roy Rogers 5" (1940's) Roy and Trigger
   "Degree" Mil Glass . . . . 129(   )10
Rose, Pete/Gold Star Chili/
   Cincinnati Reds 6" Flare . . . . 131(   )2
Show Biz Pizza Place, Mitzi 4⅝" S.S. Hvy Base . 133)   )1

Sears, reproduced catalog (1908) . . . . 135(   )1
Sonic Cars, red and white 5⅝" Libbey . . . . . 137(   )1
Sonic Silver Anniversary 25th . . . . 138(   )1
Sonic Happy Eating Sign, red-white 5⅝"
   Ind. Base . . . . 139(   )2
Space History Glass 10 oz . . . . 141(   )1
Space Scenes – Moons, Rocket Ships,
   flying saucers . . . . 143(   )1
Spokane Community College, Big Foot
   Brockway Glass . . . . 144(   )4
Sylvestor Snake – no logo . . . . 145(   )1
Taco John's – U of Wyoming, Laramie,
   cowboy's . . . . 147(   )1
Taco Time – 6" rd. btm. – no logo . . . . 149(   )1
Taco Time – 6 5/16" S.S. Hvy. Base – no logo . 151(   )1
Taco Time – 5¼" curved ind. base – no logo . 153(   )1
Tastee Freez Rainbow's & Clouds –
   no logo or date . . . . 155(   )1
Texas A & M – (1876) Seal/Sargents Head . . 157(   )1
Tony The Tiger – Hot Air Balloon (1985) . . . 159(   )1
Twitty City, Twitty Bird Playing a Guitar . . . . 161(   )0
Wizard of Oz (1989) Whataburger 4⅞" S.O.R. . 163(   )2
World Wide Arts – You can't be poor if
   you have a friend . . . . 165(   )1
World Wrestling Fed. – 32 oz. Ped. Base Glass –
   6 men on glass . . . . 167(   )1

SALESMAN SAMPLES

ARCHIES – Set #SSX

1 Big Moose
2 Veronica
3 Archie
4 Miss Grundy
5 Betty
6 Mr. Weatherbee
7 Reggie
8 Jughead

TERRY TUNES – Set #SSX

9 Heckle and Jeckle
10 Little Roquefort
11 Sad Cat
12 Deputy Dawg
13 Possible Possum
14 Lariat Sam
15 Mighty Mouse (Not a sample glass)

FILMATION ASSOCIATES – Set #SSX

16 Russell
17 Mushmouth
18 Rudy
19 Bucky
20 Bill Cosby
21 Fat Albert
22 Dumb Donald
23 Weird Harold

MISCELLANEOUS – Set #SSX

24 Frankenstein Jr.
25 Space Ghost
26 Muttley
27 Wonder Woman (1978) (Front logo)
28 Supergirl (1978)

These glasses were produced as salesman's samples. They were never mass produced and are extremely rare. 10 +

A & W ROOT BEER MUGS

CLEAR ARROW – Set #AWM
(Ice Cold)

1-49

3¼"	1(	)2
4½"	3(	)2
5¾"	5(	)2

SOLID ARROW – Set #AWM
Clear logo (Ice Cold)

3"	7(	)2
4½"	9(	)2
5¾"	11(	)2

BROWN ARROW – Set #AWM
Solid Label (No Ice Cold)

3"	29(	)2
4¼"	31(	)2
5¾"	33(	)2
5"	35(	)2

SOLID ARROW – Set #AWM
Solid logo (Ice Cold) Thin Letters

3"	13(	)2
4¼"	15(	)2
4¾"	17(	)2
6"	19(	)2

UNITED STATES MAP – Set #AWM

3"	37(	)2
4¼"	39(	)2
5½" Tankard	41(	)2
5¾"	43(	)2

SOLID ARROW – Set #AWM
Solid logo (Ice Cold) Thick Letters

3"	21(	)2
4¼"	23(	)2
5⅛"	25(	)2
5¾"	27(	)2

A & W – Set #AWM
Oval Logo

3"	45(	)2
4¼"	47(	)2
5¾"	49(	)2

MUG'S – GLASS OR CERAMIC

ALCATRAZ – Set #ALC
Mug – heavy (1977) B/W on clear glass

I Spent Time on Alcatraz . . . . 1(　)1

ALPHABET MUGS – Set #ALP
By Hazel Atlas – White Glass, square handle 2⅞"

A(　)	E(　)	I(　)	M(　)	Q(　)	U(　)	Y(　)1
B(　)	F(　)	J(　)	N(　)	R(　)	V(　)	Z(　)1
C(　)	G(　)	K(　)	O(　)	S(　)	W(　)	
D(　)	H(　)	L(　)	P(　)	T(　)	X(　)	

AMERICAN GREETINGS CORP. – Set #AME
4" White Glass #301 – Anchor Hocking

1

2

Apple Dumplin . . . . 1(　)1
Huckleberry Pie . . . . 2(　)1

CURRIER AND IVES – Set #CUR
Clear Mugs

American Homestead Winter . . . . 1(　)1
Home To Thanksgiving . . . . 2(　)1
The Old Homestead . . . . 3(　)1
Winter in the Country . . . . 4(　)1

WALT DISNEY – Set #DSC
Single Character – White Mugs – Black Pepsi Logo

2

3

4

| Daisy . . . . 1( )2 | Mickey . . . . 3( )2 |
| Donald . . . . 2( )2 | Minnie . . . . 4))2 |

WALT DISNEY – Set #DTY
Mickey, Through The Years
white mugs – blue Pepsi logo

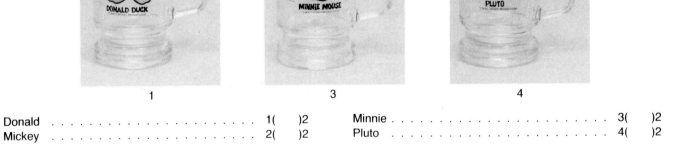

| 1 | 2 | 4 |

| Mickey – Steamboat Willie (1928) . . . . 1( )2 | Mickey in the Mickey Mouse Club (1955) . . . . 3( )2 |
| Mickey in Fantasia (1940) . . . . 2( )2 | Mickey – Today (1980) . . . . 4( )2 |

WALT DISNEY – Set #DHP
heavy ped. base – clear mugs

| 1 | 3 | 4 |

| Donald . . . . 1( )2 | Minnie . . . . 3( )2 |
| Mickey . . . . 2( )2 | Pluto . . . . 4( )2 |

WALT DISNEY – Set #DCM
Commemorative Clear Mugs

1

2

3

4

Disney Mickey Mouse Club (1955) . . . . 1( )1
Fantasia (1940) . . . . 2( )1

Magician Mickey (1937) . . . . 3( )1
Steamboat Willie (1928) . . . . 4( )1

MICKEY AND GOOFY – Set #MAG

1

2

Goofy, deserted island – clear mug . . . . 1( )2
Mickey, at helm-lighthouse – clear mug . . . . . 2( )2

MCDONALDS – Set #MCG
Garfield Series Mugs (1987)

1

2

3

4

Canoe . . . . 1( )1	Skateboard . . . . 3( )1
Hammock . . . . 2( )1	Teeter Totter . . . . 4( )1

MCDONALDS – Set #MCM
Mac Tonight (1988)

Half Moon – Microphone . . . . 1( )2
Half Moon – Large Size Mac Tonight . . . . . . 2( )2
Half Moon – Piano Keyboard . . . . 3( )2

MCDONALD'S – Set #MCO
Olympic Mugs (1984)

1

2

3

4

Back of all mugs

Blue-Sailing . . . . 1( )1
Red – Steeplechase . . . . 2( )1
White – Baseball . . . . 3( )1
Yellow – Weightlifting . . . . 4( )1

MCDONALDS – Set #MCS
Smoke Glass Mugs

1	2	3	4

Captain Crook . . . . 1(   )2
Grimace . . . . 2(   )2
Hamburglar . . . . 3(   )2
Ronald McDonald . . . . 4(   )2

ORPHAN ANNIE – Set #ORP

Annie, Daddy Warbuck's and Sandy (1982) . . . 1(   )2
Ceramic, Have a Rainbow Day (1982) . . . . . . 2(   )2
Off white with green trim top edge stripe   . . . . 3(   )2
Orphan Annie – 3½" tall white ceramic   . . . . . 4(   )2
Orphan Annie Premium Mug – 3" ceramic china . 5(   )2
Orphan Annie Revival Mug – 3½" tall white . . . 6(   )2
Sandy running for ovaltine (1932) . . . . 7(   )2

PACMAN – Set #PAC

1	2	3

Pacman Mug – (1982) Bally same front and back . 1(   )1
Pacman Mug – TM of Midway MFG–no date . . 2(   )1
Ms. Pacman Mug – (1982) Bally, blue maze on back . 3(   )1

6

8

22

24

30

Annie – Mug (1974) N.Y. New's –
white glass 3½" . . . . 2( )1
Batman and Robin Mug – 3¼" tall white glass –
red Robin/ Batwings (1966) . . . . 4( )2
Batman in black (1966) 3½" . . . . 6( )1
Billy Bob 5⅜" clear glass mug – Show Biz Pizza . 8( )1
Beatles Cup/Mug, 4" tall white pottery – BW Photo
Images of Beatles with blue jackets . . . . . . 10( )4
Burger Chef Breakfast B/C –
"It's A Good Morning Feeling" . . . . 12( )1
Coca Cola 3¾" – black and gold
"Enjoy Coca Cola" . . . . 14( )1
Donald Duck – Double Finger Ped. Base –
white 4¾" . . . . 16( )1
Hopalong Cassidy Mug – 3½" tall white glass
green picture Hoppy & Topper running . . . . . 18( )3

Hoppy Mug – 3" tall white china 4 color portrait . 20( )3
Peanuts, Snoopy (1958) UFS –
On Dog House – white glass 4 1/16" . . . . . 22( )1
Peanuts (1958, 1965) UFS – Scramblin Feet, Like Is
Pure Joy 4 1/16" – white . . . . 24( )1
Ranger Joe Ranch Mug –
3" tall white glass (1950's) . . . . 28( )3
Robin (1966) Nat. Per. Pub. Red –
action/char – 3" . . . . 30( )2

Roy Rogers Mug – 3" tall white ceramic
Roy leaning on elbows in 4 color . . . . 32( )5
Superman Mug 3¼" tall with glass – Superman
Flying Past City (1971) . . . . 34( )2
Wyatt Earp, U.S. Marshall – 3" tall white glass – scene in red
of Wyatt shooting it out with 2 cowboys (1950's) . 36( )4

NOTES

NOTES

NOTES

NOTES